FROM PRISON

A JOURNEY of FAITH

FROM PRISON to PRAISE

A JOURNEY of FAITH

BY

T.M.RAIN

and

MICHAEL HALL

Published by
Midnight Express Books

FROM PRISON TO PRAISE
A Journey of Faith

Copyright © 2014 by T.M. Rain and Michael Hall

ISBN-13: 978-0692322376 (Midnight Express Books)

ISBN-10: 069232237X

All rights reserved. No part of this book may be reproduced or transmitted in any form or by any means without written permission of the author.

Disclaimer: This is a work of non-fiction. Some names and identifying details have been changed to protect the privacy of individuals.

Published by
MIDNIGHT EXPRESS BOOKS
POBox 69
Berryville AR 72616
(870) 210-3772
MEBooks1@yahoo.com

FROM PRISON to PRAISE

A JOURNEY of FAITH

BY

T.M.RAIN

and

MICHAEL HALL

CHAPTER ONE Mike Hall

My name is Michael Alex Hall. On the street, I was known as Carolina Renegade. The name actually being my CB radio handle. I got the name from a combination of my Native American heritage, along with the state that I was born and raised in.

My father's grandmother was full-blooded Blackfoot Indian from the Kentucky-West Virginia border area of Logan County. My mother's grandmother was Cherokee Indian, and she was from the mountains of North Carolina. I was a renegade simply because I made the choice to break away from the traditional life-style of my family to become an over-the-road truck driver.

I was born in Wadesboro, North Carolina in October of 1953. At the time of my birth, my parents lived in a small, wood-framed farmhouse with four rooms and a screened in back porch. Very small by today's standards but it was enough for them, and they were happy to have what they had. Unfortunately, a lot of people would not understand that today.

I was raised up on that **small** farm and I learned to live a life that was what I will call "rugged," for lack of a better word. Our drinking water came from a well that was dug by hand. To get at the water, we had an old wooden bucket that had a chain attached to it. That chain ran from the bucket handle and through a pulley. The pulley made it easier to raise the bucket back up once it was filled with water. Hand-over-hand, we would pull on the chain until the bucket finally appeared through the opening in the enclosure. Once the bucket was raised, you had to hold the chain with one hand while trying to get a hold of the handle with the other so you could pull the bucket towards you. Once that was accomplished, you would pour the contents, what you did not spill on yourself anyway, into another container for transport back to the house. This process was repeated many times every day.

Getting water for the family might seem to some like a job to be avoided but, as a child, it was one of my favorite chores simply because, when you raised that bucket, you never knew what was going to be inside it along with the water. Sure, most of the time it was just water, but there were times when there might be a big old frog in there or, if I was really lucky, I might find a water snake in the bucket.

In the winter, our home was heated with firewood, which we cut for ourselves then hauled to the house from our land. Not only did our heat come from the wood we cut but our meals did as well since we had a wood burning stove. The wood burning stove was great because it really helped keep the house warm in the winter time but it would certainly run you out in the summer. When possible, any major cooking, like baking, would be done in the early morning hours before the heat of the day made it impossible to cook inside the house, even with the doors and windows open.

I would be willing to bet that there are a lot of old country boys like myself who can still tell you stories of waking up at about five o'clock in the morning to do their chores before school, and smelling pies, rolls, and cornbread already cooking. There might even be the smell of roasting meat for that night's supper already being cooked.

I would also be willing to bet that you will not find very many kids today who can smile with fondness at the thought of sitting at their mother's kitchen table an hour- before sunrise, enjoying a piece of hot, freshly baked cornbread and a tall glass of fresh milk that you just got right out of the cow yourself- Those are memories that made the hardness of the life we lived seem so much easier, and I would not have changed it even if I could.

From Prison to Praise

We grew nearly everything we ate back in those days. We had a small orchard of apples, pears, cherries, peaches, and plums. Dad built a grape arbor where we grew big, juicy white grapes, and dark purple ones. For kids like me, this was our candy store, and I loved it.

We had a lot of chickens running around. These birds provided us with our eggs and Sunday dinners of fried chicken. We had an old mule that we used to pull a plow and a wagon. Sometimes we would even ride the old thing.

We had cows for milk and meat. We even had hogs for our own pork. Vegetables were grown in our garden, and I can tell you right now that, even if we could have afforded to buy our vegetables in cans, they would not have tasted near as good as the ones we grew. It is like all the hours spent tending to the plants were given back to you in the form of delicious food that you just cannot buy in a modern grocery store.

And given all the chemicals used to grow "fresh" vegetables today, I am not sure I would really trust the fresh produce sold in the stores you see everywhere you go. The only chemical fertilizer we ever used came directly from the cows. Just one more use we had for them, I guess.

Yes, growing and raising our own food was hard work but it was also fun. I learned a lot about what it took to feed a family, and got a wonderful education in where food comes from. As a child, if someone had asked me where butter came from, I would not have said, "Wal-Mart." Instead, I would have pointed the person asking in the direction of my mother's old butter churn because THAT is where the best butter I ever tasted came from.

Baths were an adventure. Unlike today where you can just jump right in the shower to rinse off real quick if you need to, our bath-time was something that had to be planned out ahead of time. You have to understand that we did not have a bathroom like you find in just about any home you go into today.

On bath night, a lot of water had to be brought up from the well.

This was usually done in the afternoon so that the frigid well water could warm up a little on its own. That is one thing about well water; while it might be clean and fresh, and perfect for cooling you off in the summer time, it was not so great if you had to jump into it to get cleaned up. Especially in the winter.

When bath time arrived, which would be after supper was eaten and the dishes were cleaned and put away, a large kettle was placed on top of the wood stove. This kettle was used to heat the water that had been brought up from the well earlier in the day. Since the water has sat and had time to warm up a little, it did not take long for it to get hot on the stove. Once the water was hot enough, it was poured into a basin which you would take into the bedroom where you undressed and washed with soap and a rag to get as clean as you could.

We would take our bathes a few nights a week but it was not the only way of getting clean if you got a little extra dirty doing you chores.

We were always required to take what my mother referred to as a "bird bath," whether we felt like we needed it or not. But, during the summer, there was always swimming to be done, after all the chores around the house were finished, and that was enough to keep any kid clean. It also meant not having to pull up as much water from the well, which could get tiring after a few buckets.

I think I mentioned the fact that we did not have a traditional bathroom in our house. What I meant by that was, we did not have a bathroom in our house. At all. Baths were taken in the bedroom, for privacy but, if you had to "use" the bathroom, that required taking a little walk.

Our "bathroom," as it were, was an old outhouse, or "john" as some folks called it, and it sat down a path out behind our house about 50- 75 yards away. It was what you would think of when you think of an outhouse, being made of wood and not smelling very nice. Most of the time, I did not mind walking to the outhouse if I had to go to the toilet. I say "most of the time" simply because, if it was raining or if it was winter time, I most definitely did mind the walk, or run I should say.

Now days, some people might ask why we did not just put the outhouse closer to the main house. Well, there are a couple of reasons for that. First of all, as I mentioned a few sentences ago, it did not smell very nice. Who would want the smell of the outhouse mixed in with their mother's fine cooking first thing in the morning. Secondly, you do not want the "contents" of the hole under the outhouse seeping into the well water.

Oh, and you definitely did not want to get caught "going" anywhere close to the house. If you had to pee, and you were a good ways away from the house, well then it was alright to step behind a tree. You just did not want to get caught "going" off the edge of the porch simply because you did not want to walk to the outhouse for whatever reason.

CHAPTER TWO

My father moved to North Carolina from Ohio along with his father, mother, four brothers, and three sisters. The family lived on, and supervised, a large farm in the area. The farm had once been part of a large plantation but was, at that time, being worked by tenant farmers. Tenant farmers are people who will farm on another person s land, and they pay rent to the land owner for being allowed to do this. Sometimes the rent might be paid in cash, and at other times it might be paid with a portion of the crop being farmed; most of the time the rent is paid in a combination of cash and produce.

As the oldest child in the family, my father was not only relied upon, but expected to carry a large part of the work burden himself. Today, we might not be able to imagine a child working hard on a farm but in those days it was normal for kids like my father, and others, to be up before daylight, and working until dark. That was just how things were done in those days.

My father's family attended a small Presbyterian church on Sundays. The church was only a few miles from their home. It was at that little church where my father, Alex, first met my mother, Evelyn. Mom played the piano at the church, and she was also the daughter of a pretty well- off timber man and land owner.

My father was instantly drawn to my mother's pretty smile, shapely figure, and beautiful brown eyes. From the moment they met, my parents were absolutely convinced that it was destiny for them to be together.

Since Alex was five years older than Evelyn, and maybe even partly because his family was not quite as affluent as hers, my mother*s parents were completely against them being together. In the end, my grandparents gave in and consented to the union.

I was not an only child. I have one sister named Cathy. I never had any brothers. I can still remember my mother "being in the family way1' as it was put back then. I also remember the day my mother went into labor.

We had all just sat down for supper when "it" happened. I did not know what it meant back then, but my father grabbed me up and put me in his 1950 Ford pickup truck. He took off in a hurry up the dirt road to my grandparent's house, where I was left to stay for a while. My grandmother went back to our house with my father to tend to my mother.

I really did not mind being left behind because my Uncle Donnie, my mother's youngest brother, did not mind spending a lot of time with me. Not like today where no one wants a little kid around getting in the way.

I still appreciate the time he spent with me back then.

T. M. Rain and Michael Hall

My sister was born pre-mature. I still remember the day she came home from the hospital. We had just had a bad thunderstorm blow through the area, knocking out most everyone's power. When I was brought back home that evening, the entire house was lit up with candles burning in every room.

The newest member of our little family took up most of my mother and father's time. I was five years old then, and was used to keeping myself occupied since there was rarely anyone around for me to play with. I got pretty good at inventing playmates so I did not notice, at first, just how much of my parent's time and energy my new little sister was taking up.

Although we did not know it then, my mother suffered from post-partum depression. In those days, we just thought she was tired, which I am sure she was. My little sister needed a lot of help, even for a new born. During the first year of my sister's life, my parents would act like every move Cathy made was the most amazing event in the history of babies. Being as young as I was, I had no idea just how much of a miracle it was that she was even alive.

As she began to develop, there was some trepidation concerning her being able to learn to walk and talk normally, or at all* She was so tiny, even to the eyes of a young boy who thought everything looked larger than life, that she looked more like a china doll than a real child.

The learning process for Cathy was a long one. She was slow to start walking but she never gave up trying, and pretty soon, she eventually got the hang of it. Talking, however, was another matter all together.

Cathy needed speech therapy classes for several years before thing started sounding right when they came out of her mouth.

With all the attention my sister was getting, and with me not understanding the reason for all the extra attention, I began to experience many different changes inside myself; both emotional and mental. I went through feelings of being "somewhat less than favored," all the way to feeling "kicked to the curb." Not saying that this was how I was being treated or anything like that, it is just how I felt like I was being treated. Chalk it up to the mind of a child.

In response to these feelings, I began to respond in various ways. Whenever I was feeling sorry for myself, I would pout for hours at a time.

I would do things to get attention, including misbehaving and doing things that I knew I was not supposed to do, or not doing the things I was expected to do. In the end, all any of this did was get me into trouble, and that was not the kind of attention I liked getting.

After a while, I decided to try a different approach. I decided that, instead of doing things that got me in trouble to try to get attention,

I would try being the best at everything I did to get the attention I felt like I was missing out on. After all, I reasoned, who does not like a winner.

My father was a very hard worker. Even as a small child, I knew this to be true. I decided that if I were going to get my father's attention I was going to have to work as hard as he did. My father always told me that a real man was not afraid of a little hard work so, I would become as hard a worker as he was.

One of my daily chores was to make sure the wood box by the stove always had plenty of wood in it. I began stacking to wood so high that I had to use a chair to reach the top. This pretty much went without notice until the day a piece of wood fell off the top and landed on my mother s foot. Instead of a compliment, I was told I need to be more careful when stacking the wood. This did not deter me from my mission. I just made a mental note to be sure that I made the stack of wood as secure as I possibly could.

Another effort I made to gain my father's attention and approval was, not only did I do my chores the way I was supposed to, but I would try to do a little extra work to try to take some of the pressure off my father who did most of the work around the farm anyway. This did not go without notice however, and my reward was my father figuring out that since I was getting older, and showing him that I could handle even more work around the place, then I could handle a few more chores added onto what I already had to do every day.

When I began school it did not take long for me to learn that a good, or bad, grade on my report card seemed to make my mother and father take notice. With this knowledge, I studied hard so that I could bring home the best report cards of anyone in my class, which was not all that big to begin with.

There were only fifteen kids in my first grade class. Most of them were girls. YUCK! We began each day by reciting the Pledge of Allegiance then the teacher would read something from the Bible and say a prayer. This was before certain groups started protesting God in school and made the school systems stop allowing this practice.

During this time in my life, going to church was very routine for my family, as well as most of the families in the area in which we lived.

The church was a very small Presbyterian congregation. It was located very close to our home which allowed us to walk to services on Sundays during the summer, if my mother felt like walking. Those images play out in my head like a Norman Rockwell painting. Just the mental picture of a young family dressed in their Sunday best, walking down an old country road, makes me want to go back to those innocent days of my youth. I can almost feel my parent's hands holding mine as we walked, my father carrying Cathy in his arms, and my mother carrying the family Bible.

At the church, my mother still played the piano, just as she always has ever since learning as a girl. There was a children's Sunday school class that I attended, and enjoyed greatly, as a boy. The Sunday school teacher was an older lady, maybe in her 50's, and she would bring graham crackers for everyone as a snack. I do not remember her name now but I do remember how she was able to hold all of our attention with the Bible stories she would read to us. She was always ready and willing to answer any questions we had about what she had read us, and she did it in ways that was understandable even to small children. I loved Sunday school.

The grown-ups had their own Sunday school, and I had no idea what theirs was like, but I just assumed it was like the one I went to, Cathy went with my folks to there Sunday school since she was just a baby.

After Sunday school, we had Church where everyone gathered in the main part of the church and the preacher would hold the Sunday service. Since I rarely understood anything the minister talked about,

I would try to come up with other ways to occupy myself, like trying to use the few reading skills I was developing in first grade to read the Bibles that were in the little cubby holes in the pews in front of where we sat. I did not understand anything I was reading anymore than what the preacher was saying but it gave me something to do, and kept me from getting into trouble. Something I was trying to avoid by then.

One of my favorite parts of Church was the singing. We would sing a lot of hymns during the services. I would sing as loud as

I could and this always seemed to make my mother happy. I would look up to see her smiling down at me from where she was playing the piano and singing. My mother always had the prettiest voice in the church and I always imagined that God himself was taking time off from everything else he was doing those days just so he could listen to Mom sing.

As much as I liked to hear my mother sing, I also liked it when my father would be asked to close the service in prayer. To me, this was a great honor, and I was always proud when Dad was chosen for the task.

I can remember swelling up just a little and stand so close to Dad that my shoulder was touching his leg. I even stretched so that I stood a little taller too. I wanted anyone who happened to be peeking to know that this was MY dad who was closing the service.

After service, I would run outside to play with the other boy or two my age who also attended our church. We would run around playing tag while the grow-ups caught up on all the gossip. In those days, people went to church for more than worship. Church was something of a social event too. Many people did not get to see or talk to one another like they do these days. There was no Facebook or Twitter. If you were lucky enough to own a telephone then I guess you could keep up with what was going on better than most. For the rest of the people out where we lived, you went to church to see what everyone else was up to.

Church was also where you went if you needed help with something. If your barn needed repairs and you could not afford to have a carpenter fix it, you went to church to ask for help. If your neighbor had been sick and unable to work, you went to the church and everyone pitched in to gather food or whatever else was needed for the ailing individual.

Of course, there were people who were too proud to ask, or even accept, help from the church or anyone else. These people looked at asking for help along the same lines as asking for charity. While they were more than willing to help others, they just would not accept anyone else's help.

On more than one occasion, the men of the church got together to take food, clothes, money, or any combination of the three to someone who was in need, but not willing to let anyone help. They would take the donations that were collected, sneak up to the person's house, and leave everything on the porch. When Dad would get home, his eyes would be bright, shining, and alive with excitement and joy over the caper they had just pulled off.

We stopped going to that church a few years after Cathy was born because it merged with another church then finally closed. My mom, sister, and I started going to church with my grandmother. It was a Methodist church in town, close to where I went to school.

My father did not attend the new church with us all that much. He said he had to work those days, and sometimes he would be in bed asleep when we returned from church. It would be around this time frame when I began to notice my father having the smell of whiskey on him occasionally. Sometimes I would even catch him sneaking a drink then hiding his bottle.

In those days, we did not have television so our news (what we did not get at church) and entertainment came from listening to the radio. Adults made the children leave the room or house so the grown-ups could talk back then. Because of the culture and life-style of the day, I did not know much about adult business back then.

When I was in the fourth grade, something terrible happened. The President of the United States was shot and killed. It was a very sad time but not for any reasons I understood. I mean, I knew it was sad that someone had been killed; I just did not understand how much that president meant to people of all walks of life.

CHAPTER THREE

Two years after the assassination of President Kennedy, everything seemed to be going really well for my family. Of course, I did not know it then but, this was just the calm before the storm.

For a long time, my mother had dreamed of building a new house. Mom and Dad had found a design they liked, and they had even found a contractor to do the construction. Mom began to obsess over every little detail of the house. Everything had to be just so because what they were building would not only be a statement of whom my parents had become, it would be their reward to themselves for all their years of hard work.

While plans were moving forward on the house, I was old enough that I would go to the river with my uncle on Sundays to fish rather than having to go to church with the women. We would leave out before daybreak and spend the day drowning worms. This was my statement that I was becoming a man because men had more important things to do than be dragged off to church by their mothers on Sunday morning.

About the time school started back, my mother had worried and fretted over the plans and building of the new house so much that she had become sick. It was just too much for her along with all she did at home taking care of the family, I was starting the sixth grade that year, and little did I know, my world was about to come crashing down around me with little or no warning at all.

My mother had to go to the hospital suddenly. When I asked about it, I was told that she was just exhausted from all she had been doing and needed to rest. This seemed reasonable to me because I knew my mother worked every, bit as hard as my father did. It was at school however that I began to hear other things.

One afternoon I was asked why my mother was in the nut house. Yes, kids can be cruel. The fight that followed was the first real trouble I had ever been into. The boy that made the mistake of making such a terrible verbal attack (as I perceived it) on my mother was older, and definitely bigger, than I was. But I failed to take notice of that small detail at the time.

After school, I invited the boy who felt like spreading rumors about my dear mother to step behind the school house with me. The altercation that ensued did not end very well for him. It took some time for the principle to make it there to get me off of him. No one else was willing to try to step in to break us up because I was taking out all of my anger and frustrations on this kid. I remember screaming and crying while I beat and beat this kid. There was spit running out of my mouth and blood running out of his while I hit him with everything I had. I must have looked like I needed to go to the nut house myself that day.

The principle, once he got me off the kid, took me to his office and gave me a paddling. This was in the days when teachers and principals could do that sort of thing without someone losing their minds over it.

Normally, a paddling would be enough to make you have all the regret in the world for whatever it was you had done to get it. In this case however, it was more than worth it to me.

My dad worked near-by then so the principal took me to my father's work and told him what had happened. After the principal left, my father, being the fair man he was, asked me for my side of the story. I told him what had been said by the other guy about Mom. Then Dad asked me about the fight. I admitted that I was the one to throw the first punch, and that the other guy never even had a chance to even hit me once. When I was finished with my story, Dad thought for a few minutes then said that since I was paddled at school, he figured

From Prison to Praise

I had been punished enough for one day. To this day I still believe I saw a slight glimmer of pride in his eye when he sent me on my way, with a warning not to be fighting at school anymore, that is.

Over the next couple of years, my parents separated several times before finally ending their marriage in divorce. I will not go into the reasons for any of the separations or the divorce because those are not my stories to tell.

As a teenager, I was attracted to a girl who went to my school. Like my own mother, she also played piano at her church, and I began riding my bicycle about five miles to her church every Sunday just to see her.

Of course, since she had my undivided attention, I heard little of anything that was being said in Sunday school class or by the preacher during regular services.

During the third week of August that year, her church was

having a week-long revival service, and she invited me to attend. I thought this was a good deal for me because I would get to see "Her" every night, from Sunday through Friday. What I did not know was, the "good deal" was going to be something even bigger.

Sunday night started the revival. I sat in a crowded area close to where the preacher was standing so that I could catch an occasional glimpse of the young lady who was the whole reason I was there to begin with. Something about the preacher's voice kept drawing my attention away from the girl and I found myself listening to the message for the night. There was just something interesting about what he had to say that seemed to draw me in, just like it seemed to be drawing everyone else in.

Before the preacher closed the service for the night, he had "Her11 play a song while he gave an invitational. For reasons I could not explain, this caused me to become very uneasy. I sat there, hoping the feeling or invitation would end soon. At the time I chalked it up to just wanting to get to talk to her, but maybe it was something more.

The next night was even worse. I got to the church a little early in hopes of seeing the girl I was there to see in the first place, but she was nowhere to be found until she showed up sitting at the piano looking like an angel herself. The service started and let me tell you what; that preacher sure did know how to make a fellow feel bad for the things he had been doing.

By the third night, I had to hold on real tight to the back of the bench in front of me to keep from going up there. By the fourth night however, I could not hold out any longer. He had gotten to me with his talk of the Father's love, and the sacrifice Jesus made for me, for all of us, on that cross. I had been doing wrong for a long time. I knew that God was not pleased with me because I had been drinking, cussing, telling dirty jokes, and doing a lot of other things that I thought would numb the pain I was feeling inside. I was a 16 year old boy who was growing up too fast, and I needed something more in my life.

I could not wait any longer. I got out of that seat, walked to the front of the church, and made a profession of faith right then and there.

I asked for forgiveness for all the wrong I had been doing and made a vow to change my life and live the way Jesus would want me to live. I felt the weight of the world lift off my shoulders that night.

I joined that Baptist church and became very hungry for all that I could learn about Jesus and the Bible. I heard sermons about miracles and forgiveness. I heard the preacher tell the congregation that, no matter what, we should never doubt God and if we trusted in Him, He would always lead us through anything. I saw this in action a year later.

I had a very good friend, my very best friend actually. I will call him "Billy" for the purposes of this story, Billy normally drove to school every day since he was lucky enough to have his own car. Not something common in our area in those days. On this particular day, Billy had four girls with him the day he left school to go home. He usually carried a few friends home on his way so they would not have to walk. Unfortunately, they never made it. Billy and two of the girls were killed when they were involved in a wreck.

The other two girls ended up in I.C.U. for quite a while but they eventually pulled through. Barely, I know it had to be hard for the parents of the girls who died to deal with their loss, I could not have imagined what that must have been like. What must have been even harder were Billy's parents having to suffer through not only the loss of their son but they also had to deal with the anger and grief of the other families involved.

I was in shock myself. I had never had to deal with such a

tragic situation before, I was not sure how I was supposed to feel or act. If I laughed at something, I felt guilty for feeling anything but sadness.

If I cried, I felt like I had no right to show sadness for the loss of my friend when his parents were suffering the loss of a son.

Even through my own confusing emotions, I knew God was there with all of us. I watched Billy's parents walk of faith and drew inspiration from them. I knew that if they were going to make it through this then so was I am sure that Billy's parents had many questions for God after the accident. One of them being, "Where were you when my son died?" That is the question any parent would ask. I also know without a doubt in my heart that God's answer to that question was, "The same place I was when my son died. Waiting with open arms to welcome him home."

CHAPTER FOUR

I graduated high school the following June then began working two jobs until the end of that year. Then I started attending Columbia Bible College in South Carolina. Although I was living in South Carolina during the week so I could attend classes, I still lived in Polkton, North Carolina as well.

The following summer, I started a summer job at Polkton Manufacturing Company. This was a sport shirt manufacturer who sold most of their product to Kmart stores across the United States. I was working in the stock room in the shipping department then. This was when I met the cute little blond who would become my wife. I will call her "Noreen."

Noreen, as I said, was very cute, and she got my attention the moment I first laid eyes on her. She also worked for Polkton Manufacturing, in the production department. She worked as a shirt folder, and the department she worked in was right next to the shipping area where I worked so I got to see and talk to her often. Within the year, we were married.

Being married and attending school out of state was not a very good combination so I decided to drop out of Columbia. Once I dropped out of there, I began attending Wingate University, which was near Polkton, and only fifteen minutes from our home.

At this time, I was very active in the church. I did a little substitute preaching at the church Noreen and I attended, and when given the chance, I preached at few of the other churches in the area. I also worked all the overtime I could, and once I felt financially secure enough, agreed with Noreen that it was time to start our own family.

The first child we were blessed with was our son, David. He was perfect and beautiful and I could not wait to have another baby. Of course that did not happen right away. Actually, it would be two and a half years before our next child came along. This one would be our daughter, Tammy, who was just an angel.

Eventually my priorities started to get mixed up. Church and school started getting put on the back-burner because I need to be at work, trying to "get ahead" so I could take care of my family. Little did I realize at the time that in trying to do what I thought was right for my family, I was actually losing them.

It got to the point to where I never went to church anymore because I had to work. I could not take Noreen or the kids anywhere because I had to work. Vacations? Nope, I had to work. "I have to work" became my mantra. It was my excuse for everything and, honestly, I thought I was doing the right thing. How could I possibly think that I was doing "the right thing" by turning my back on my family, church, and God, you might ask? I have no excuse. It is just what I did, and my marriage of four and a half years fell apart because of it. And so did I.

After losing Noreen and the kids, I was very angry and bitter. I could not understand why God had allowed this to happen after all I had done for him and the church over the years. I worked hard, I never cheated on my wife, I made sure she and the children had everything they needed. This had to be God's fault, I reasoned, because I certainly had been doing everything right. At least that is what I convinced myself of. I was in so much pain over the loss of my family and, what I perceived as, God turning his back on me that I started to drink. Heavily. It was the only thing I could think of to do that might have a chance at helping to deaden the pain I felt. I no longer cared about anything. Getting ahead at work did not matter, church certainly did not matter to me, and the drinking was not much of a help either. I needed something else to take my mind off of my troubles.

I decided that the best way to get away from the pain I was in was to get away from where the events happened. I had to get out of town, and the best way to do that was to become an over-the-road truck driver.

I got a job driving truck and stayed on the road as much as I could. Slowly the pain started to go away. Not all the way, but enough for me to be able to function again as a "normal" human being. I credited the fact that I was always driving with the way I was feeling. Not happy, but not hating life so much anymore. When I was driving, I was thinking about what I was doing. Keeping my eye on the road. Thinking about where I was going and where I would go after that. The destination of the next load became my world. Not one time back then did I worry about the destination of something much more important; my soul.

It was the driving that kept my mind off of my crumbling and crumbled life. I did not like to sleep because I would think, and thinking never got me anywhere. Or no where I wanted to be, anyway. To keep driving, I started using drugs. Stimulants became my new best friends. Yellow Jackets and White Crosses were taken by the handful, and coffee as thick as motor oil was poured down my throat by the quart. I did not think there was anything wrong with what I was doing since the pills kept me awake and alert rather than being sleepy and dangerous. In truth, had someone brought it to my attention, or if I had been honest with myself back then, I probably still would not have cared. I needed to drive. I needed to run from the pain. I needed help.

Miles and years passed. Sometimes I started to see what was happening to me, what I was doing to myself. Sometimes I did not care. I started attending church again a couple times, but I could not forgive God for what I thought he had done to me, so I would quit going, and start drinking again.

From Prison to Praise

I was on an emotional roller coaster and I could not get off, even when I thought I wanted to. Eventually, I met someone. I thought she was a gift from God; someone to make up for the family that was so unfairly taken from me, as I had come to think of it. Of course I was only fooling myself again and that marriage ended badly, and quickly. I decided I was ready to return home, so that is what I did.

Since I stayed on the road most of the time, I had actually been able to save a little money. I was not rich, but I had enough to last me for a while if I was careful with my spending. Of course, to me, being careful with my spending meant buying whiskey by the gallon instead of by the pint. It was cheaper that way.

I do not know what I thought I would find by returning home. I was a heavy drinker and I had quit my job. I had two divorces under my belt and my prospects for the future were not looking very bright. Some days were good however, and I could spend those days going to the river to fish with a buddy, which I did not have many of by this time. Few people could stand to be around me for very long, and I could not really blame them. I had a lot of hate in me, and this made me a very bad tempered drunk. If I could come up with a reason to start a fight with someone, that is exactly what I would do, whether I thought I could win or not.

As you can imagine, along with those good days, I had very bad days.

My dark days, as I call them. It was during one of these so-called dark days that I got my first DWI. I did my little time in jail, paid the fine and court costs, then went right back to what I was doing. A little splotch on my driving record was not going to slow me down. I ended up with another truck driving job despite the DWI arrest. I did not stay on the road as much as I did the first time, however. This time I tried being at home whenever I could get there.

During one weekend home, which was rare because I was low-man on the totem pole at the trucking company and that meant I had to make all the weekend runs, I ended up in jail again for DWI. I would not be so lucky this time because this was my second arrest in as many years, I lost my driving privileges for the next four years because of the arrest, and my job with it.

Now do not start thinking that this is what it took for me to "see the light," because it was not like that. I simply moved on to the next thing. I started my own business.

Since I was always good with my hands, I decided I would open a shop selling tires and rims, and doing automotive repair work. This was stuff I was good at, and since there was a room I could live in in the back of the shop, I would not need to drive to get to work. This was a win-win situation for me. At least I thought it would be.

I am not going to say that a drunk cannot run a business, but I will say that I had a little trouble running my business, and keeping customers. When I woke up in the morning, I had a drink. When I opened the shop, which might have been at normal opening time (7:00am), or it might have been at lunch time, I had a drink or two. When there were no customers waiting, I had a drink. If someone had dropped their car off for me to work on, I might have a drink before I got started. If I was frustrated with trying to fix something that wanted to be stubborn, I would drink and think about it. If I was frustrated over not having many customers, I would have a few drinks and try to figure out what the problem was. Needless to say, I was drinking A LOT. Then I started smoking marijuana when I drank. I was going downhill very fast, and there was no sign that I was going to start slowing down any time soon. As a matter of fact, my life was about to start to spiral even more out of control than it already was. And I would not have even imagined that was possible.

T. M. Rain and Michael Hall

CHAPTER FIVE

There was a young lady who worked at a small convenience store where I would go to buy my beer. She was attractive, and a nice person on top of that. Since the weekends were long and boring, I made arrangements with the little lady to go with her to a club in a nearby town. This helped me in a couple of ways; first, i did not' have to drive, which kept me out of trouble. Second, it gave me somewhere to go, something to do, and someone to do it with. I would usually pay for gas, and I would buy her drinks while we were out.

What began as a mutually beneficial arrangement soon turned to marriage number three. Mabel, my new wife, already had a son when we got married.

His name was Dustin, and he was two years old when I married his mother. Dustin had red hair, just like his mother. After a couple of years, our marriage was going pretty good and Mabel and I had a son together. This was Dylan.

We began going to church some, just not as regularly as I used to go.

I also still had a little resentment in my heart because of the past so I did not make church a priority. If I had something that I felt like was better to do on a Sunday morning, then church was out that week. Eventually, things happened and we stopped going all together.

I was not drinking as much as I once had but we did drink and smoke pot some, especially if we had friends over or we went to some else's house to party. It was at one of these parties that someone first turned me on to "crank." of course, as a truck driver, I had heard a lot about crank, or "road dope" as a lot of drivers called it, but I never tried it. Even as far out as I was on the pills and alcohol, I was still afraid to try a drug as hard as crank. But, these were different days, and I was still looking for something to fill the emptiness I still felt inside.

I figured crank might be just the ticket. So, I gave it a try.

I snorted a line of the white powder and it burned like I had snorted hot coals straight from the bonfire. For a few seconds I was wondering what I had gotten myself into, and why anyone would want to do this to themselves, especially after they tried it the first time. Soon the burning stopped and the high began.

The crank, or meth, which is what it is called these days, high was not like anything I had expected. Well, to be honest, I am not sure what exactly I was expecting but it was not like what I was feeling. I had a ton of energy, and I did not want to sit still. I looked for things to fix, and occasionally fixed things that were not broken. I did not sleep much, and I all but quit drinking because I soon learned that I could not get drunk when I was on crank.

Crank was my new drug of choice. When I was on it, I felt

happy. I could concentrate on work, and if Mabel and I were having any personal problems, we could do a little crank then sit and talk things out. For hours!

Mabel and I soon started to develop a new circle of friends. If you did not do crank, chances are we did not have time for you. Not saying we completely blew off our old friends, we just did not make time for them. If someone who did not do crank stopped by to visit, we were cordial enough to the person. It was just that we often felt like we no longer had anything in common with most of our pre-crank associates.

As my use of crank grew, so did my connections in the subculture that went hand-in-hand with the use of the drug. What began as a one-night party soon turned into days, and even weeks, of heavy use. To afford our drug use, I began buying small quantities, then splitting it up and reselling it. I made enough to cover my investment and personal use, which seemed to be growing by the day.

Arrest was inevitable, and I knew it. That is just part of the drug "game." If you play, you will eventually have to pay. I know that sounds like a cliché, but, hey, what can I say?

Seriously though, I knew I was playing a serious game when I started dealing drugs. I had a family to lose, again, along with my business, and what little good reputation I was slowly getting back in the community. I needed to be careful, but as we all know, no one is perfect, and in November of 1999 I was finally arrested for possession of a small amount of methamphetamine. I spent two days and nights in jail.

In the area of North Carolina where I lived, crank was known, it just was not very common. The people where I lived who knew anything about crank, or who had at least heard of it; thought of it as a biker drug.

Sure, all the guys and girls who drove semi-trucks knew more about it than most people since crank was, and still is, a very popular stimulant in the truck driving world. But to local law enforcement, the use of crank was not much of a "problem" in the area yet. As far as the police were concerned, crank was a West Coast problem, basically confined to California and places close to there. Although crank had been making its way east for several years, it was still thought of as a novelty in my town. Therefore, if a local got arrested with any of the stuff, the police and judges pretty much gave them a slap on the wrist, and a warning not to do it again.

Law enforcements laxity when dealing with crank arrests made it hard for me to take such an arrest seriously. Because of this, I found myself in jail again the following February on my second crank arrest. Once again, I did not take the arrest seriously, thinking I would be out in a day or two. That did not happen though. Apparently, someone was starting to see that crank might be a little more of a problem locally than they might have first imagined. I was not going anywhere for a while. At least until law enforcement had time to do a little investigating.

Almost daily I was questioned about where I had gotten the drugs I was caught with. I told the investigators that I had picked them up somewhere along the road back when I was a truck driver and that what I was caught with was just some that I had found still stashed in my travel bag. Of course they were not falling for this story but I was not going to change it so they had no choice but to believe me. That is, not until April when I was busted the third time with crank. And this arrest happened while I was still in jail!

I was not actually caught "with" any crank, I was just noticed to be acting strangely, one of the jailors thought I was high so he pulled me out of the cell and took me to see the nurse who ordered a drug test.

It came back positive for methamphetamine.

I was placed in solitary confinement after the drug test came back.

Since I would not admit to where I had gotten the drugs, they decided to keep my in a cell by myself, "for my own safety," they said, what they did not know, and I was not about to tell them, was that there was just as much crank in the jail as there was outside on the streets. I was pretty skinny, because of my crank use, when I came into the jail that I was sure no one even noticed that I was not eating most of the time. When you are on crank, you rarely eat. By the time they caught on to what I was doing, my addiction was even worse than it had been before I came to jail.

Being in solitary confinement was difficult for me. I had no access to anymore crank so I was forced to dry out. I think this was the whole purpose of locking me away in a cell by myself to start with. Whatever the reason, it was during this time that I was able to get clean for the first time in a long time.

The cell I was left in for my solitary time was small, and very uncomfortable. There was a bed with the thinnest mattress I had even seen, and this was even by jail standards. There was a toilet and sink, and the temperature was kept somewhere around Alaska in early spring. I was miserable.

One morning, while the jailor and trustees were passing out breakfast trays, I asked if there was something around that I could read. I had read my toothpaste tube so many times that I could recite the entire label from memory. The jailor said that he would see what he could do.

When the trustees came back to pick up the empty food trays I was already back in my bunk, under the covers trying to get warm. I heard a heavy thump on the floor when my tray was picked up so I peaked my head out from underneath the thin blanket and saw a book laying on the floor of my little cell. It was a Bible.

I picked the Bible up, and began to read it. It had been a very long time since I had actually "read" the Bible. What I mean is, you can read something and not get anything out of it. You read the newspaper and get a little information and that is fine. You can do that with the Bible as well. You can read it and get a little information. But, if you open your mind, your eyes, and, most importantly, your heart, and really READ the Bible, you get so much more out of it. This was something I had avoided doing for so long that it took me by surprise when God actually started to speak to me through what I was reading. I started to see that every one of my problems were my own fault, not God's.

The things I was learning, and admitting to myself for the first time in a long time, were very hard for me. I knew what I had been doing, the life I had been living, was wrong, and I knew, deep down, that the reason I was doing it was because I wanted to blame someone other than myself for all the years of pain I had suffered through. I wanted to blame God.

I started praying and telling God that I was sorry for everything.

Even thought I knew that God knew everything I had been up to, I still searched my memory for all the wrong I could remember doing, and I ask for forgiveness for each of those things individually. Then I begged to be forgiven for all the things I could not remember doing.

Before long, I started playing "Let's Make a Deal," with God. I told God that if he would help me out of this trouble I was in, just this once, I would get my butt back in church and start living and doing right. That was it. I made the offer then I waited for God to answer. A couple of months later, a got my answer when I was released on probation.

CHAPTER SIX

My homecoming was very emotional. I did not realize how much I had changed until I walked out of that jail feeling free in more ways than one for the first time in many years. I felt like there were possibilities open to me now that had never been open to me before. I was ready to start my life over, with Mabel and the kids, and I knew that no matter what happened from here on out, God would be in charge, and everything would be alright.

Mabel and the kids had already been attending church with her father while I had been away in jail. At her invitation, and the invitation of her father, I began attending church with them. We were at church every time the doors opened. If there was something going on, or something that needed to be done, we, Mabel and I, would be the first to volunteer to help.

This time however, my time at the church did not take away

from my family. This time, everything we did at and for the church, we did as a family.

There were certain groups and classes in the church that Mabel, the kids, and I would attend separately though. The boys had their kids Sunday school classes, Mabel had her ladies groups, and I like to attend the Tuesday morning Bible study group, which was lead by the Pastor's wife.

The group was made up of several other men and women, and I really enjoyed the time we spent going through the Bible, and hearing what the others got out of the verse we were studying. It always amazed me how eight people could find eight different meanings in a single verse.

One morning before the start of our study group, the Pastors wife made an announcement that she and the Pastor would be going out of town the next two weekends, and the week in between. This meant that there would be no one there on

Tuesday to lead the study so she wanted to know if anyone wanted to volunteer to lead the group while they were away? I sat there expecting one of the more senior members of the group to step up, but when no one did, I spoke up and said I would be more than happy to take over for the next meeting.

I felt good about getting to lead the next study group. It was a small thing, but it was something that I felt would bring me a step closer to God.

On the following night, at the Wednesday night service, the Pastor said he wanted to speak to me before I left. After service, I met up with the Pastor outside. He had another congregation member with him and when I walked up to them the Pastor told me that I need not worry about "going out of my way" to lead the next Bible study group. He said the person standing with him was going to lead the group, and I thought this was odd because this person was not even a part of our regular group. But, I said that would be fine with me, thanked the gentleman and the Pastor, and went home.

Mabel's father stopped by the next morning and began apologizing to me for what the Pastor had done. I assured him that it was not an issue whether I lead the group or not, just so long as someone was there to do it. He looked at me a little strangely then said he was not worrying about who lead the group, he was upset over the reasoning for the change being made after I had already been told I could lead the group, I told him I did not know there was a "reason" behind it. Sure, I supposed the Pastor and his wife wanted someone with as much Bible knowledge as possible to head the study, but that was as much thought as I had put into it.

Apparently my trials would not be over. As it turned out, the reason I was replaced as temporary leader of the Bible study group was because, according to the Pastor, I was not a "member" of the church. I was stunned to hear this, and the more I thought about it, the angrier I got, and the more it hurt.

I wanted to go confront the Pastor, and not in a good way. I was furious over his prejudicial attitude. I mean, it was okay for me to give my money to his church (tithes and offerings). It was okay for me to volunteer my time mowing the grass and weed eating, painting, sweeping, and taking out the trash. It was not enough to be at every service and to travel, at my own expense, to other church's activities that our church was helping with. None of that mattered at all. The only thing that mattered was that I had not signed this Pastor's church membership card! I almost could not believe this.

As much as I wanted to let the Pastor know exactly what I thought about his policies, I did what I knew was the right thing to do; I wished him the best of luck and all God's blessings then I stopped attending that church. Mabel, however, kept attending because she was a member, as were the children. I did not ask her to stop going simply because I felt like I had been slighted unfairly by the Pastor. She was free to worship where she felt comfortable. I also did not blame God for this latest turn of events either. The Pastor was a good man; a Godly man. I just did not agree with his policies so I left of my own accord so I would not feel uncomfortable there, and neither would anyone else. I knew God would show me where I belonged, and He would do it in his own time. Until then, I studied my own Bible, with Mabel joining me from time to time. I did not need to be in a particular building to feel close to God. If I could do it in a tiny jail cell, I could do it in my home, surrounded by the family I loved.

A couple of months later, I was finally invited to attend another church in the area. I only knew a few people who actually attended this church, but everyone seemed friendly and welcoming. I attended regularly on Sunday mornings and

Wednesday nights, and I made sure that, once I felt like this church was the place for me, I signed a membership card.

* * *

I felt good and secure in the fact that my relationship with God was being renewed. I could feel Him working within me, and I knew there was something that He wanted me to do. I just did not know what exactly that "something" was going to be. But, being a patient man, I was willing to wait as long as it took to find out.

One thing I know, and have always believed, is that God knows what is truly in our hearts. We can lie to ourselves, we can lie to our friends and families, but we can never lie to God, Anyone who thinks differently is just fooling himself.

God knew my heart back then. He knew that the commitment I had made to him this time was for real. And it was forever, regardless of whatever came at me in the future. I no longer had the desire to do the things I used to do to try to forget my pain, or to try to feel loved. I knew that God loved me now, just like He always had, and I knew that I could stand up and take anything thrown at me, as long as I stood with God.

These were the things I KNEW, not just believed, and I was about to get my chance to prove my faith in God's wisdom was absolute.

One Sunday morning, I felt like I needed to do more for God. I had done so much against him that I suddenly had this overwhelming urge to want to make up for the mess I had made of the good life He had once given me. Sure, I knew He had forgiven me, and I knew that the new life I was living was a gift from God that I would not let slip through my hands again so easily. I just felt like there was more that needed to be done, and I felt like God wanted me to do it.

That Sunday morning I went to the alter and totally surrendered to God. I told Him that I knew that there was something He needed me to do, even though I had no idea at this point what it was. So, I just prayed for Him to use me however and wherever it would be most pleasing to Him.

Three months later, God let me know what his need for me was, and it was not anything that I could have imagined.

I had gotten ready for work that morning just like I always did, getting dressed, then having a cup of coffee and a bite to eat. At 6:30am, I walked out the front door to leave for work, and that was when I noticed two strange cars coming down my driveway at a relatively high rate of speed.

My pulse quicken as I stood there because, as I said, these were strange vehicles, and they were driving like they were on a mission. I was afraid something terrible had happened to someone, like an accident, and these were people coming to tell me about it.

Both cars slid to a stop right in front of where I stood. All the doors (both cars were 4-doors) flew open and men dressed all in black jumped out. Each was carrying a small, black assault rifle, and they were pointing them at ME! I began to panic because I was having a bit of trouble mentally processing what was happening. I started to back away from the men, and what I was beginning to perceive as a direct threat to me health, to say the least. This was a mistake, I think. All the men started yelling at me, telling me to do different things. Some wanted me to get on the ground; some wanted me to put my hands up. I was told to turn around by someone; and someone else told me not to move or he would shoot me. I was terrified and did not know what to do at all so, I did the first thing that came to mind; I just stood there.

Finally, somebody figured out who was supposed to be in charge and one of the officers approached me. He grabbed my shoulder and lead me to the front of one of the cars; he forced me to bend over the hood of the car, then began to search me, placing all of my belongings on the hood next to me. I was then handcuffed and read my rights. I was going to jail.

The officers who arrested me would not speak to me. I tried asking was going on, but they refused to tell me anything except for the obvious fact that I was under arrest. 1 asked WHY I was under arrest but was told I would have to wait until we got to the jail before I could find out what the formal charges were. Finally I decided to stop trying to get information out of the officers. I decided to speak to a higher authority so I began to pray.

T. M. Rain and Michael Hall

CHAPTER SEVEN

I spend two long days in jail without learning a thing about what was happening to me. I was not told what the formal charges were when we got to the jail, like I was told I would be. Finally, on the third day, I was taken to a courthouse I had never stepped foot in before. This was a Federal Court, and I had a sneaking suspicion that I was in serious trouble.

Once I was brought into the Federal courthouse, I was taken to a small room where I was photographed and fingerprinted again. The Federal Marshall who was taking my photo and fingerprints was very respectful to me the entire time but he, like everyone else, refused to tell me what was going on. When I asked, he just said that I would have to wait until I talked to my lawyer. When I said that I did not have a lawyer, he simply said, "You're about to get one." Then he began taking photographs of my tattoos and scars.

After the fingerprinting and photographing and questioning, I was lead to a cell that was made entirely of stainless steel. The walls were all stainless steel, as were the benches, the door, the sink, and the toilet. There was something else in the cell I was not expecting to see; people I had not seen in a long time.

Walking into that cell that day was like taking a step back in time to my drinking and drug using days. Just about everyone I used to party with was there, and there were several people I did not know but everyone else seemed to know. I asked around to see if anyone knew what was going on and was told only that the Feds were the ones arresting us. No one seemed to know WHY they were arresting us though, but I was about to find out for myself.

After what seemed like a long time, but was probably only a couple of hours, a court officer started coming for us. He would take us out of the cell, two at a time, and he would cuff us then lead us away through a door at the other end of the room in which the cell was located. After a while, he would come back for two more, never bring any of the others back with him.

When it was finally my turn, I was cuffed and lead away with one of my old "friends." We were lead through the door, and out into a long hallway. We walked to the end of the hallway then we were loaded into an elevator that had a cell inside it. The officer did not lock the cell but he did pull the door shut before letting the elevator door close.

We rode the elevator up to the third floor where we were put into two new cells, each of us in one of the cells. There were only two cells and none of the others were there either. I still did not know where they had gone, and this only added to my anxiety.

It did not take long before another court officer came to get us.

The first one did not take our cuffs off when he put us in the smaller cells, and this one did not seem inclined to take them off before he led us to wherever it was he was leading us to. This would be the actual courtroom where we would be meeting the judge, and finally finding out what we had done so wrong as to attract the attention, and wrath it would seem, of the United States government.

If you have never been inside a Federal courtroom, I can tell you that it really is a sight to see. You have never seen so much solid cherry paneling, chairs, tables, and other items of furniture as I was seeing in that one room. One HUGE room, I mean. This room covered so much area that, if a lawyer needed to say something to the judge or the prosecutor, he had to speak into a microphone to be heard. It was, to me, a blatant waste of tax money.

I was directed to sit at a table where there was a man in a suit.

From Prison to Praise

The "friend" with me was directed towards another table, where another suited man was sitting. These would be our court appointed lawyers for the duration of our case.

My lawyer introduced himself and said that once the hearing was over, he would try to make it by the jail to see me within the next few days.

I asked if I was going to be allowed to post bond to get out of jail and he looked at me like I had said something completely ridiculous. The lawyer said that this particular hearing was simply to have our charges formally read to us. Any consideration for bond would come at a later date. As you can imagine, I was not happy about not getting a bail hearing but at least I was going to find out the reason I had been arrested.

Historical conspiracy dating back to January of 1999, or before that date, for the manufacture, sale, and/or delivery of methamphetamine. That was what I, along with fourteen other people, was charged with by the U.S. government. Now that I had the big question answered, I was ready to move forward with the case.

True to his word, my new lawyer came to see me a couple of days after the court hearing, when the hearing was over, I was rushed out without time to say anything to my lawyer. Obviously, I had questions, lots of them, but he stuck his business card in my pocket, and said he would be around to talk to me. Before I was able to respond, a pair of hands was pulling me towards yet another door, where I was loaded into yet another elevator. That elevator took me to the parking garage where I was put back in the police car that brought me to the courthouse, and then I was brought back to the jail. Now I was sitting there across a small, wobbly card table from my new lawyer, and he seemed to be a little more relaxed.

I am guessing that he knew little or nothing about my case

when we first met, and now he had had the opportunity to read a little more about it, and was ready to pass information on to me.

My lawyer told me that my charges stemmed from my past drug history.

I kind of figured that, but what I was having trouble figuring out, and he was no help in answering this, was why were they just now coming after me? I had been away from that life for a long time. I had cut ties with everyone from that life. I was no longer a drug user, or associated with drugs or drug users in any kind of way. The lawyer told me that he would try to find out as much as he could before his next visit but, going from his experience, he guessed that someone who knew me had probably gotten busted then told every name he knew in order to cut a deal to save himself. It did not matter, my lawyer said, that I no longer made, sold, used, or delivered drugs. What mattered, to the feds anyway, was that I once had, and someone apparently told on me for doing it. Now what I was going to have to try to do was minimize the damage and hope for the best.

As hard as it might be to believe, I had remain pretty calm throughout all of this, trusting that, what I had committed to God, He was in control of, and I did not have to understand it. I just had to keep my faith and believe God had a plan for me and this was part of it. I had peace.

Something else about being indicted by the Federal government is that, once they have you in their custody, they will bounce you around from jail to jail, holding facility to holding facility, over and over again, and for no apparent reason. That is something that was happening to me but, instead of resenting them for this, as most inmates did, I used the travel as an opportunity to talk to other guys about their relationships with God.

Psalms 37, verses 23 & 24 say,

> *"The steps of a good man are ordered by the Lord; and he delighteth in his way. Though he falls, he shall not be utterly cast down, for the Lord upholdeth him with his hand."* (KJV).

That passage was one of many that God used to speak to me, and it was also something I tried very hard to pass on to my fellow inmates. God speaks to us all, all of the time. Whether we choose to listen or not is entirely up to us. Many of us, myself included, normally only hear him when things are going good for us. We look at our good fortune as a blessing from God, and most of the time, that is exactly what it is. But God also speaks to us during the worst of circumstances, and that is when we should be listening closest.

It is difficult to try to get someone to look at incarceration as anything other than bad luck, or "The Man" being out to get him. These are not only negative thoughts, but they are the most common. Prison is Satan's playground. He whispers in the inmate's ears, causing them to think God has turned against them. This in turn makes a lot of inmates begin to blame God for their misery. I would not let this happen to me.

From the day of my arrest, I remembered that I told God to use me however and WHEREVER he needed me. If prison was where he needed me then that is where I needed to be.

In our county jail, I was placed in a cell block that was made up of fifty two-man cells. Each cell consisted of a set of bunk beds, a stainless steel sink, and a stainless steel toilet, that the sink was actually a part of. Kind of a 2-in-1 thing. Our meals were delivered to us through an opening in the door. This opening was commonly referred to as the "pie hole," or "bean hole."

From Prison to Praise

The cell block I was being housed in was a 23/1 block. What this means is, we were allowed out of our cell for one hour a day. The remaining twenty-three hours, we were locked down. During the one hour of recreation time that we were allotted each day was when we were allowed to shower, and exercise, phone calls could also be made at this time, but those calls had to be made collect. The only problem really with this being the only time we could use the phone was, you never knew what time you would be allowed out for your hour of recreation, it could be as early as 6:00am, right after breakfast, or it could be as late as 5:00pm, right after dinner was served. With this problem of never knowing what time you might be able to call home, your family would have to sit around and wait for your call, if they wanted to talk to you. If they had to work, or go somewhere, they could miss you and you would not get another chance to call until the next day.

Something that I always noticed, no matter where I was in jail, was that there are always certain inmates who are "in" with the guards. These inmates can get the guard off to the side and tell him that they would like to be let out for their rec. time at a certain time of day. The next day, the guard would be sure to let them out when they had requested.

That meant that there was never any real system to keep track of when you might get out the next day, unless you knew someone had asked for this special favor and you knew what time they had asked to be let out.

The recreation area was secured by two locked doors that lead into an inner hallway traversing the perimeter of the facility. Needless to say, none of us were going anywhere unless the guards wanted us to.

For security reasons, all of the inmates were not allowed out for recreation at the same time. The guards would open ten cells at a time while the remaining forty cells remained secured. Day time was very noisy because everyone had so much energy to release after being cooped up for twenty-three hours. Also, inmates would go over to their friend's cells who were not let out yet, and they would talk to them through the door. Shout to them, is a more accurate description actually, because the doors were made of thick steel so you had to yell to be heard.

I had little luck in jail when it came to talking to anyone about God. When everyone was out, all they wanted to do was get their showers, use the phones, talk to their friends, or do push-ups. It was frustrating to me that I could not get anyone to sit down and talk about what God's plan for us might be. Surely God has a plan for everyone, I believed then as I still do today, so why would someone not want to try to figure out what that plan is, and how it effects him? I was starting to wonder if it really was God's plan for me to try to reach others; in jail anyway.

In the "dayroom" there were stacks of books that inmates were free to take back to their cells to read. I searched the stacks until I finally came across an old Bible. I figured I needed to study more to figure out what I needed to be doing to please God since it did not look like I was going to be able to help any of my fellow inmates find their way to the Lord.

My roommate slept most of the time so this meant I could read and study without being interrupted. Not saying that I did not want to talk to him, I just did not want to talk about the things he always seemed to want to talk about. He knew that one of my charges was for manufacturing meth, and he was always asking me questions about how to cook it. I had no desire to teach a "cooking" class, and figured that this guy constantly trying to draw my mind away from God and back to the very thing that got me where I was at that moment was nothing more than Satan working on me. I chose to ignore his questions, and would offer to tell him what I found more fulfilling that any drug I ever used, but he was not interested in hearing it, so he slept.

King Solomon, who wrote Proverbs, was given great wisdom in all things by God. Considering where I was, and not knowing yet exactly what God wanted from me, I opened my Bible to Proverbs to start my reading. I knew that, given the fact that the choices I had made more than eight years earlier were what had landed me right where I was at, my choices were not always what you might consider "wise." With that being the case, I figured I would try learning from a wiser man than I.

Once I had found Proverbs, I said a prayer, asking God to tell me what I was supposed to be doing, what was his plan, and how could I serve him?

I looked at my Bible and it was opened to the third chapter. Verses five and six nearly jumped off the page they became so real to me. I read:

> *"Trust in the Lord with all your heart and lean not unto your own understanding, in all your ways acknowledge Him and He shall direct you."*

Once again, I was reminded of the commitment I had made to God just a few months earlier. I trusted that God had a plan for me, but I really thought that plan might have something to do with me helping others find or renew their faith. Once I had done that, I thought God would help me get out of this mess I was in. Surely, I thought, God could not possibly be planning on keeping me locked up; could He?

This passage was so clear, and frightening, to me. I thought I knew what God wanted from me, and I was getting frustrated with myself for not being able to deliver. But now I was thinking that a short time in jail was not God plan at all. He needed me for much more. "Trust in the Lord with all your heart." I had trust in the Lord, of that I had no doubt. Where I found myself starting to struggle was in wondering WHERE it was God was about to direct my path.

By this point in my life, I had a wife and two teenage sons at home. I was partners in a logging business, and I had been very active in my church. Also, I had a little granddaughter that brought me so much joy.

How, I wondered, could God take me away from all of that? Why would he do that to me? I was bombarded with a whole new round of questions, doubts, fears, and worries to which I had precious few, if any, answers. This time, I was not about to give in to despair. This time I went back to my Bible, knowing the answer would be found in God's word, if nowhere else.

T. M. Rain and Michael Hall

CHAPTER EIGHT

This time, instead of picking a spot in the Bible that might scare me even more, I decided to start my reading where most people start; at the beginning. I opened to the book of Genesis and read until I came upon a story that caught my attention.

This story was about someone who had spent a considerable amount of time in prison. His name was Joseph. Because of his incarceration, I felt a connection to the man, however, unlike me, Joseph had been falsely accused, yet he was in prison just the same.

While Joseph was in prison, he was able to maintain his faith. He trusted in God, and never compromised his integrity. Knowing I was not innocent, I was finally starting to see how God might be able to use a man such as myself just the same. I began to pray and I acknowledged to God that I was willing to follow whatever path he set out before me. He just needed to show me where to start.

Now that I had made peace with the fact that I would not be going home anytime soon, something wonderful happened; I went home.

I was sent home on pre-trial release to await my day in court, where I would stand before the judge. I was closely monitored during this period by an ankle monitor. This was basically house arrest since I was allowed time to go to work and church, but otherwise I had to be at home.

I was not permitted to attend any extra church functions, or any other activities. With this limited amount of freedom, I was able to spend as much time as possible with my family. Time that I knew was limited, and time I knew I would cherish the memory of once I returned to jail. And that day was coming even sooner than I expected.

Along with the probation department, who was in charge of

monitoring me while I was out on pre-trial release, I also kept in constant contact with my lawyer. He was working hard to try to get me a good plea agreement from the prosecutor's office. The last I had heard from him, he said he could get me a deal where, if I agreed to plead guilty to all charges, I would receive a sentence of 42-60 months in Federal prison. I did not like it but, from everything I was learning, five years was a good deal for all the charges I had.

The day finally came when my lawyer called to tell me that I needed to meet him at the Federal courthouse that was about one hundred miles away from my house. I was there on time and the lawyer took me into a small room where he presented me with a plea agreement to sign. Like I said, I was expecting to agree to a sentence of 42-60 months. I certainly was not prepared for what was sitting in front of me at that moment. The numbers of the page I was looking at stated a sentencing range between 188-235 months.

This was the most devastating day of my life. Nothing could have prepared me for this. Tears welled up in my eyes as I began calculating what I was looking at. Someone was asking me to agree to sign a plea agreement that would send me away for 15-20 years. I was 55 years old at the time. All I could think was, "My life' is over."

With the knowledge that I would be around 70-75 years old by the time I was released, I began to panic. I felt like someone who was drowning and I struggled to find a way out. Unfortunately, according to the man sitting across from me holding the ink pen out to me for me to sign my life away, there was none. Well, that is not entirely true; I had the option of going to trial where the Feds have over a 90% conviction rate. If I went to trial, I stood a good chance of being sentenced to twice as much time WHEN I was convicted.

As my shaking hand took the pen, I silently prayed, "Lord, help me."

With the signed plea in his hand, my lawyer told me to wait while he took it to the prosecutor to get signed. As I waited in that little room, I started thinking about the story of the three Hebrew men that were sentenced to be thrown into a fiery furnace. I wondered how they felt on the day of their sentence. Was it anything like how I was feeling?

I thought I could understand their fear, seeing as how I knew my life was over too, at least as far as I was concerned.

I drew strength remembering that, because they trusted God, they were not in the fire alone. In fact, the King who had ordered them to that fate saw a fourth man in the fire with them. I knew then that I did not have to worry. Just as God was with them; he would be with me as well.

As I was called out of that room that day then taken before the judge, I knew that God was right there with me. What I did not know was that this was the end of my freedom.

This meeting was just supposed to be for me to sign, or turn down, the plea agreement sent to me by the prosecutor's office. If I signed it, which everyone knew I would, I would go before the judge and he would decide whether or not to accept it. Sentencing would not occur for several months. The judge looked the papers over then asked me a few questions.

Once he agreed to accept the plea, I was ordered to be returned to custody immediately to await sentencing. I would not be going back home.

I was taken back into Federal custody, and placed in a Federal holding facility. This place had twenty-four two man cells, and was a lot different from the normal county jail. This place held nothing but federal inmates, and since we were all going through the same thing, there was more of a brotherhood-type environment to the place. It was also a lot quieter since most everyone there had more important things on their mind than seeing who could yell the loudest about who won the previous night's game on the television.

This facility did not keep us locked down twenty-three hours a day either. This meant people were apt to talk to you simply because they had more time to burn off their extra energy, and little activity in which to do it. I began talking to this one individual about the Bible.

When he saw that I was somewhat knowledgeable about what it said, he asked me if I would care to sit with him at a table in the common area and explain to him what he was reading. This quickly turned into a daily Bible study and prayer group in our cell block. The group met every evening at 6:00pm, and the number of attendees varied from four to twenty-six men.

Saturday afternoon was the weekly visiting day. There was a room on the second floor where two or three men could get visits at the same time. The room had a glass partition that kept the visitors separated from the inmates. My wife and boys came nearly every week for the 20-30 minutes we got to visit in the strictly controlled environment.

On the first Saturday in August, I was waiting for my "people," as we call our families, to come visit. My wife had assured me that she was bringing the boys, and when she told me she was going to do something, I always knew that I could count on her to do it. That, along with God's love, was one of the very few things I knew with absolute certainty I could put my trust in. That is why I was really beginning to worry when 4:00pm rolled around and I still had not been called up for visit.

Finally, at 4:05pm, two hours later than I was used to my people getting there, I was finally called for my visit. I hurried to the visiting room, and when I walked in, my wife was not there; only my oldest son, Dustin.

I sat down across from him and started to ask him where his mother and brother were, but he cut me off. "Dad," he said, "I have some bad news I have to tell you. Just as I was about to leave to come down here, we got a phone call from your step-dad. Your mom just died."

That was devastating news for me, and certainly nothing I was expecting to hear. It was not even anything that I had thought about happening while I was locked up. Sure, I considered the fact that, due to my age and the amount of time I was looking at, I might never walk out of here alive, but I never thought about any of my loved ones passing on while I was incarcerated.

I talked to my son for a while, and while we visited, dinner was served in the unit. As news normally does, the news of my mother's passing spread quickly. By the time my visit was over, everyone in the unit knew what I was just finding out. I guess one of the guards told one of the trustees who told a couple people in the unit who told everyone else.

At the end of the visit, I walked out of the room and headed down the stairs. As I did I could feel forty-six sets of eyes following every move I made. It was unusually quiet in the unit then. I guess no one really knew what to say or they just wanted to see how I was going to react to the news.

When I got to the common area, one of the guys from the prayer group told me that he had my dinner tray so I went to join him at his table. While I ate in silence, he said that he was truly sorry to hear about my loss. This was a sentiment shared by a lot of others as well. I guess being around someone who suffers a loss such as this really brings it home to those around him that they too can lose someone they love while they are incarcerated.

Something that a lot of people do not realize is, when they are living a life of sin, drinking, and using drugs, it affects those around them in a lot of different ways. Once we, my fellow inmates and I, got caught for what we had done, we were not going to be the only ones who would have to suffer.

Even though it had been several years since my drug days, I was going to have to pay for what I had done. I knew that there was a chance I would never walk the streets again as a free man. That was my cross to bear, as they say. I guess I just never took into account how much my family was going to have to suffer along with me. Up until this point,

I just thought they would hurt because of my absence and because they would worry for my health and safety. But there were other issues as well.

My family, in the midst of my legal trouble, was now having to deal with the loss of one of our own. The matriarch of our family was gone.

My family needed me and I could not be there for them. My son was burdened with delivering news to me that I should have been giving to him. I should have been out there letting my mother know just how much she meant to me before she died, but I wasn't. Now that I had this new way of looking at things, I knew that the knowledge of my families suffering was always going to be part of my punishment.

When I sat down to my dinner, my prayer group brother said that the group was only going to meet for a quick prayer that night since they figured I would not feel up to teaching that night. I shook my head in agreement for a second as I chewed my basically tasteless food. I had not thought about the group yet, and maybe I did not need to be trying to teach anything to anyone when my mind was occupied with other things. That was even what I was about to say, but when I opened my mouth to say it, something else came out instead.

I said we would meet, as always, at 6:00pm. This response came from somewhere deep inside me, and I barely even heard myself saying the words but, once the words were out, I knew it was what I really needed to do. I needed to speak to the guys about what I was feeling, not keep it all inside as I sat alone in my cell, feeling sorry for myself. There was a lesson in all this, and I wanted to share it with my brothers.

That evening, our group was exceptionally large. I think everyone in the unit attended. I guess they just wanted to hear what I would have to say. I knew that everyone had already heard about my mother, but I told the group again anyway, so they would be hearing it directly from me. This is a good policy in jail because rumors spread fast, and the truth gets lost in the telling just as fast.

I spoke to the group about how I was feeling about the loss my family had suffered, and how it would affect all of us. I spoke about my mother's faith in, and love for, God. I remember sharing with the group that, as a result of knowing I would see my mom again one day, because she was a Christian too, it took away the finality of her death. It gave me peace to know this, and I was able to smile as the power of this belief flooded through my body.

My family made several phone calls trying to make arrangements for me to be at my mother's wake and funeral. Due to several factors, like the fact that I was a Federal inmate, and being held in a Federal holding facility in Dillon, South Carolina and the services would be held in Wadesboro, North Carolina, it was going to be a next to impossible task.

The only thing that the holding facility would agree to was letting me go to the funeral home in the presence of two guards. I would be handcuffed the entire time, and I would be required to wear the bright orange jail jumpsuit we had to wear at the facility. I would be allowed FIFTEEN minutes in the room with her, but only AFTER it had been cleared of all other family members, then secured by the officers, who would be with me the entire time.

On top of it all, I would be responsible for paying, in advance, the costs for the officers, their overtime, their food, transportation, and any other additional fees the administrators could think of. Although my family was willing and able to pay the costs of getting me to the funeral, I declined their generosity. My reasoning was very simple: my mother was always an honorable lady. To go through the preposterous steps required for me to get to see her for a few brief moments would have brought dishonor and embarrassment to both our family and her memory.

I spoke to my wife and sister, before and after the memorial service. It was described to me as being a beautiful service that was very well attended and tastefully done. I was very moved when I was told about the graveside service. A pigeon, representing Mom's spirit, was released. Three others, representing the Father, Son, and Holy Spirit were also release at the same time. The four birds joined together and flew away. This was symbolic of what Paul spoke about in his letter to the Church in Corith:

> *"To be absent from the body is to be present with the Lord."*

Answering the question of what happens to a believer after death.

My days continued as usual, and I continued to follow my normal routine in the holding facility of walking an hour a day. It was the most exercise I could get. One day a young, black gentleman in the unit, I will call him "Ray," asked if he could walk with me to talk. I knew who Ray was, and I knew about his crime.

Ray was a gang member, the Bloods to be exact. He was known on the street, and in the holding facility, for being tough and very violent. He was not the kind of person you wanted to attract the attention of.

Ray was in the holding facility awaiting trial for taking part in the beating of a man that was so severe the victim barely survived and was not expected to ever be able to walk again. Ray was very proud of his charge, and bragged about what he had done every chance he got. Needless to say, him wanting to talk to me made me a little nervous but I could tell that there was something bothering him, so, I told him I would be more than happy to walk with him.

We walked in silence for a couple laps around the unit. I did not know what Ray had going through his so I just kept quiet until he was ready to talk. Finally, he asked me how I could deal with the death of my mother like I was. He told me that there was no way he would be so calm about it, like I seemed to be; stating that they would have to come take him out of there in a straight jacket if it had been his mom. I knew I felt a peaceful calm about my mother's passing, I just did not realize that it was showing in a way that other people could see it.

1 began to share with Ray the source of my strength. I explained to him that, if all we had in this world was HOPE, then I would be a very miserable person. He did not seem to understand so I said that, if all I could do was walk around and hope my mom was with Jesus, then I would have doubt as well. That doubt would drive me crazy.

Because of the sacrifice made by Jesus Christ, the hope and doubt are gone. It is because Jesus Christ, the first-fruits of the resurrection, lives that I have confidence my mother's live as well.

I have faith that I will see her again, and I know, as a Christian, that I will get to spend eternity where they are today.

I asked Ray if he knew where he would spend his eternity if he should die today. His response was that he had not really given it any thought. Since I had long ago come to understand that, all the time we spend alone gave our minds a chance to process the deeper subjects we might not feel comfortable talking about all at once. I did not want to push Ray on anything, or try to rush him into thinking about something as important as eternity. I wanted him to come around on his own. No one can make us come to God. That is something we all do in our own time, and in our own way. I planted the seed with the question I asked. Now I just had to wait for it to take root, if it was going to.

Ray did not talk to me for a couple of days after we talked. Then, one day, he joined me again as I was walking. He talked about his life on the street, and what it was like for him growing up. He told me, and I was sure this was not something he shared with very many people, that he was often awakened during the night with nightmares about some of the things he had done. Ray truly was a tormented soul.

I would walk with Ray as long as he wanted. Sometimes he would just go on and on about whatever was on his mind. On those days, I would just listen. Some days, he was full of questions. I would answer anything he asked, as honestly as I could. And, I tried to keep my answers simple, so that he did not get confused over any finer points I was trying to make.

Not to say Ray was dumb, he just had a very limited education, and an even more limited knowledge of Biblical matters. I wanted to spark his curiosity, not scare him off.

Ray still seemed confused over the inner peace I displayed around the unit. I explained that it was all very simple. Yes, I loved and missed my mother. But, I knew I would see her again one day. It was more like she was gone on a long trip, or moved away. One day I would pack up and move to where she was at, too.

As Ray silently contemplated his own eternity, I began to explain to him how I had come to know Jesus Christ as my own personal Savior, and how I had made Him Lord over my life.

One day while we walked, an idea struck me. I asked Ray if he was under the authority of anyone else in the gang of which he was a part of. He explained to me a little about the structure of the organization, and how it all worked. There were guys who were higher up in the 'family that were directing many of the groups actions and activities. They were in charge of the lower members as well. The gang had power, and they used this power to control those around them.

I asked Ray if his gang had any enemies. He looked at me a little funny then assured me that they did in fact have many enemies. I asked him if he knew who all of his personal enemies where, and he said that there were way too many to keep track of them all. Then, I asked him if he was aware of the fact that he was an enemy of God. Ray stopped dead in his tracks and stared me down. I could tell I had just shaken him, and I am sure that is not a feeling this man was used to feeling. I asked him to come sit with me.

We found a place where we could talk, and I began to explain to Ray that, because of the life he was living, he was in total rebellion against God. Everything God did not want him to do, he was doing. Every commandment given to use through Moses, he had, most likely, broken.

He was an enemy of God, and it was by his own choosing. It did not take long, but Ray started to understand what I was telling him.

I went to my cell for a moment then returned with my Bible in hand. I opened it to Genesis, and showed Ray how God had created the world and everything in it in six days. Since God made it, I explained, it belongs to Him. We were all living on God's turf.

I went on to show him how God had created mankind in his own likeness. He gave us dominion over the earth and over all creatures great and small. He also gave us something no other creature had; a soul.

God gave us the ability to think, to reason, and to choose. With this ability to choose, it became our choice to open the door of our heart, and invite Christ in to take up residence. God, in His greatness, created mankind to have a relationship with, and he gives us this assurance: He will never leave us or forsake us.

That day, I had the privilege of leading Ray in a prayer of

repentance toward God, and as he placed his faith in Jesus Christ as his personal Lord and Savior. As the tears rolled down from the eyes of this powerful young man, I felt as though I was witnessing a living miracle. The dead being raised back to life.

Ray was very hungry for knowledge, and wanted to learn all he could about Jesus. We had just been provided new Bibles that had been so generously donated by the Gideon's. Ray was one of the first in line to receive one. Although he could not read very well, and had a hard time understanding what he was able to read, he still spent several hours every day in private study.

He joined our 6:00pm Bible study and prayer group. Always full of questions about what he was reading, our Bible studies often turned into good natured philosophical debates. Ray never shied away from joining in these debates, flexing his newly acquired mental muscle, and interjecting his views where he thought he could without embarrassing himself.

I became amazed at the complete change that was taking place in Ray.

No longer was he the bully who used his size, strength, and reputation as a ruthless thug, who gave up no ground, to demand and get the things he wanted, the way he wanted them. Another, unforeseen, benefit to having Ray in our prayer group was that we no longer had to endure snide remarks occasionally tossed our way by the unbelievers in the unit. The lion in the den might seem tamed, but everyone was smart enough to realize that he was still a lion.

Brother Ray starting showing how thoughtful and kind he could be. Where he used to take what little the weaker among us had, he began to give to those who had little, or nothing at all. He became a living testament to what Paul wrote in 2 Corinthians 5:17:

"If any man be in Christ, he is a new creature; old things are passed away. Behold, all things become new."

Due to our location (jail), and our circumstances (we were inmates), our group was continuously changing as guys went to court, were sentenced then shipped out, and new people took their place. On a Monday morning, Ray took his place as one of those leaving to face whatever the future, and the Lord, had in store for him.

It was early when they called for Ray to pack out, a couple hours before breakfast, if I remember correctly. After he had his things packed up, Ray stopped by my cell to wake me up, and to say good-bye. We prayed briefly, and before Ray left, he thanked me for helping to lead him to God. He also promised me that he would continue to serve God, no matter where he ended up. I believe in my heart that he meant what he said, and that he has kept his promise.

CHAPTER NINE

The afternoon after Ray's departure, he was replaced by another young man. His name was Manuel.

Manuel was from Mexico, and he spoke very little English. Through another Spanish speaking individual, I was able to learn a little about Manuel's story.

Manuel had come to the United States illegally in search of work. He had a wife and daughter, who were still in Mexico, living with his mother. Manuel worked hard, taking any jobs he could find, to earn money which he sent back to Mexico to his mother. She used the money to care for herself as well as Manuel's wife and child. That is, until he was arrested. Manuel's crimes were driving without a license and being in the country illegally. The latter being a federal crime. By the time I met Manuel, he had already been bounced around from county jail to county jail for over a year.

He was also a Christian, and very committed to his faith. Although we could not communicate as well as we would have like, Manuel and I became friends. We would sit and read our Bibles together. We were able to acquire a Santa Biblia (Spanish Holy Bible) for him.

From time to time, as we each read our Bibles, we would come to a passage that we felt had great personal meaning to us. In order to overcome the language barrier, we used an elaborate, but effective, jumble of hand signs, pointing, and broken English/Spanish phrases to share God's word with one another.

The more I got to know my new friend, the more I learned that he seemed to be most moved by two subjects. The greatest was the love of God towards all men, no matter who they are, where they are from, or what they had done. It fascinated Manuel that God could see through all the bad people do to one another, and still love each and every one of us equally.

Although he did not talk about it, I felt like Manuel had seen a lot of bad things being done to people by others. He would tell me that, where he came from, it was very beautiful, but men made it an ugly place. He seemed very sad about this, so I can only imagine what he meant.

The other thing that really moved Manuel was, the future being in God's divine hands, which according to one passage he pointed out to me, "He holds the heart of the kings, and turns them whichever way He would have them go."

Manuel was very knowledgeable about the Bible, so it was a surprise to me to learn that he had only been a Christian for about eight months, in that time, he had already read the Bible through twice, and continued to search the pages over and over again for nourishment in which to help his spirit grow.

Through an interpreter, Manuel often shared in our Bible study and prayer group, inspiring truths from the reading he had done. On one such evening, during our Bible study, two new men arrived in our unit.

Both appeared to be Mexican, but they could have been from any other Spanish speaking nation. With a smile on his face, and a twinkle in his eye, Manuel got up from the table and headed over to meet the new guys.

Oscar and Franko were the newbies. Manuel went to work on them right away, building familiar ties, and by the next evening we had two new members of our Bible study group.

That is just how it was at the Dillon County Federal Holding Facility, people were always coming in and leaving. Those arriving were often looking for something to cling on to. Like a drowning person trying to grab a hold of anything that floats, people were willing to try anything if they thought it would save them.

"Jailhouse Religion," is a term used for people who come to

jail and find a sudden interest in God that they never had before. Often these people will attend every Bible study, church meeting, or prayer group available, thinking that it will save them from whatever the courts have in store for them. A lot of these guys will have beautiful, new, leather bound Bibles sent in that they can show off to everyone else, yet they never crack it open to take advantage of the treasures held within. I have even witnessed people using the pages of their Bibles as rolling papers for their cigarettes

Not everyone who comes to jail and starts to worship God for the first time is suffering from jailhouse religion, however. A lot of the people are just as serious as those who have been raised in a good Christian home their whole lives. I guess that it is just like anything else; you have the good and the bad. For this reason, no one in our prayer group ever turned anyone away if they wanted to join us. Even if they walked away from our table, dropped their Bible on the floor, and started playing cards at the poker table. We still welcomed them to join us in the hope that something would go with them when they walked away.

A guy called "Buckshot," a nickname pinned on him from the damage done to his left arm, side, and leg, was brought into our world one day. He began his stay as so many new guys do, by acting like he was a hardened criminal, afraid of no one or anything. This is a common defense mechanism that anyone who has done much time has seen a hundred times over.

Eventually, Buckshot began to mellow out and we began to talk. As I figured, he was just hurting inside, and was scared and unsure of what lay ahead for him. I assured him that what he was feeling was no different than what any of the rest of us were feeling. I invited him to join our prayer group one night. He did, and at his request, we prayed for God to give him the strength and guidance he would need for making for making the choices he was going to have to make, which were going to so greatly alter his life. He walked away with more peace than he had walked in that unit with, and with that, we knew God was at work within him.

The "Rev" was an interesting guy, and I must tell this story before I go any further. Most Saturday mornings, meant one thing to us, the Rev was coming. With his eye catching suits, and his powerful messages that actually required you to think about what you were hearing, he was a very popular guy.

It was a normal Saturday morning after breakfast when the call came: "Rev's in the house!" Guys started hitting the doors to come out for the service, which was always held in the common area. This day he was wearing an electric blue suit with shoes to match. I am not even sure I had ever even seen that shade of blue on a suit before, or since.

The Rev was so dark black that the contrast seemed even

greater than it actually was.

As we gathered around the tables we knew that whatever message he was bringing today would fill each of us with encouragement, conviction, and hope. On this particular day, his message was from the Book of John, chapter eight, verses one through eleven, where a woman was brought to Jesus. This woman had been caught in the act of adultery and the religious leaders had brought her to Jesus to test Him, by seeing what He would do.

Jesus stooped down and began to write on the ground with His finger. Then, he looked up and looked around at all of the religious leaders standing around Him and said, "He that is without sin among you, let him cast a stone at her." Jesus looked back down and started writing on the ground yet again. From the oldest to the youngest, those who had brought the woman before Jesus started to leave until the only people left were Jesus and the woman who had been accused of adultery. Looking around, Jesus asked the woman where those that had accused her went.

She told Him that there were none left. He then told her that He did not condemn her either, and that she should "Go, and sin no more."

Rev's message was simple. He was letting us know that Jesus loved us and would forgive us but He expected us not to go back out into sin again. After closing in prayer, Rev had a challenge for us. We were to try to determine WHAT Jesus wrote on the ground with His finger, and to be prepared with our answers the following Saturday.

Unfortunately, no one in our group had anything more than the plain Bibles that were supplied to us by the jail. None of them had a cross reference section or a concordance to use to aid us in our quest for answers. We were all going to have to do this the "hard way." Father, help us.

Each day and night we searched for an answer. The Rev's question was the topic of discussion at every Bible study session, where we shared and discussed our various ideas and possibilities. That Friday evening, as I sat on my bunk reading from the Prophet Jeremiah, I came upon a verse that nearly knocked me over. In the Seventeenth chapter, verse thirteen, I read:

> *"O Lord, the hope of Isreal, all that forsake thee shall be ashamed, and they that depart from me shall be written in .the earth, because they have forsaken the Lord, the fountain of living waters."*

Those religious leaders had sought to trap Jesus rather than recognize Him for who He really was. But, when He turned the tables on them, they hung their heads in shame and walked away rather than having to address the sin in their own lives.

To me, it seemed as though what Jesus did was write their names, and maybe even their sins, on the ground that day.

The next Saturday I was anxiously awaiting the arrival of the Rev. Finally, the call came, "Rev's in the house !" He walked in wearing a bright red suit and matching shoes. Before he could even begin talking, one of the guys asked him if would mind telling us the answer to what Jesus had written on the ground.

The Rev told us that it could not be proven, but he was convinced that the scribes and Pharisees Jesus was addressing knew the law and the prophets. He was referring to the Old Testament portion of the Bible. They would have been required to have committed it to memory. Rev stopped then and asked if anyone in the group before him had been able to find the answer for themselves. When it seemed that no one had found an answer to the question, I slowly raised my hand.

Rev pointed a finger at me and boomed, "Wait!" His voice was so loud that it seemed to rattle the steel doors of our cells. Everyone was quiet as Rev looked at each individual person, never taking his finger from my direction. When he was certain that no one else had an answer, he smiled at me and lowered his arm.

The Rev paced for a second before he began to speak again. He told us that the previous week when he asked us the question, God had spoken to him. Rev said that God was going to give the answer to the question to one man in this building, and that man to whom the answer would be revealed would be an anointed servant of God, called and set apart for God's work.

Rev asked me to stand, which I did, feeling every eye in the place on me. Then he asked me if I truly had the answer, and could I back it up with scripture? I said that I could. I told the group how I had been reading Jeremiah and how the passage had come to me as brightly as if it were a neon sign, brightly illuminated against a background as dark as a black velvet night.

The Rev became more excited than I had ever seen him get, and I have seen him get pretty worked up before. He broke out into a kind of dance, as he raised both his voice and his hands towards Heaven. When he started to calm down just a little, he returned his attention to me. He came rushing back in my direction, one hand stretched towards me, the other reaching into a pocket on the inside of his suit. In all honesty, I was beginning to get a little freaked out over his reaction, and I did not know what to expect when he pulled a small bottle from his pocket then told me to close my eyes.

He placed his hand on my head and began to pray. As he prayed and spoke to God, he was pronouncing His blessing over me for the service God had called me into. Then he poured out the contents of that bottle, anointing me with oil. When he did that, it was as if something new flowed into me, causing a warm, euphoric feeling like none I had ever felt before. Somehow, I knew that this was God's blessing I was feeling.

CHAPTER TEN

That night, after the Rev had come and gone, I lay in my bunk thinking about what had transpired that morning. The sudden rush and high I had felt initially had worn off, although I did continue to feel a little "different" somehow. I felt almost as if I knew where my future lay, and what it was I had to do, even if I did not know exactly HOW I was going to do it.

That was when the attacks began. Suddenly I was bombarded with doubt. Not just doubt about what Rev had said, but about what I was feeling also. I began to ask myself, "Was it just the emotion of the moment?

Was I just caught up in the sensationalism of Rev's presence? Was I just riding the wave of his enthusiasm? Who did I think I was to believe God would want ME for anything special?" Question after question ran through my head, and eventually I began to pray for some kind of understanding. That is when I picked up my Bible, feeling almost drawn to it.

I opened my Bible to Luke, because that is what we would be discussing the next day during Bible study. I started reading in chapter four, and when I started reading about how Jesus had been tempted by Satan for forty days, I was thinking that he must be attacking me in a similar manner.

No matter what Satan did, Jesus always defeated him by simply using the power of His word - the Bible. WOW! The same weapon Jesus had used against Satan was in my hands, and I was determined to use it to stop the attacks Satan was using to try to bring doubt upon me, and the calling I knew God had bestowed upon me.

To me, it became evident that Jesus' earthly ministry started after he was "tested." He returned to Nazareth and went to the synagogue on the Sabbath, as was His practice. He stood up to read from the scrolls of the prophet Isaiah, and this is what he read:

> *"The Spirit of the Lord is upon me because He has anointed me to preach the gospel to the poor. He has sent me to heal the broken hearted, to preach deliverance to the captives, and recovery of sight to the blind, to set at liberty them that are bruised, to preach the acceptable year of the Lord."*

It was like a light had been turned on inside of me. Suddenly it had become so real. Even before my incarceration, I had been in prison, held captive by my circumstances, as I had sought for freedom through alcohol, drugs, hard work, relationships with numerous women, and any other illusionary form of escape I could think of. I had continually spiraled deeper into despair, ultimately bringing me to where I was at that moment.

I knew that God had placed a calling on my life many years

ago, but even now I caught myself wondering if I had not blown my chances just by the life I had lived for so many years? Surely I had so damaged my credibility with the life that I was living that no one would believe anything I said, if they were even willing to listen to me in the first place.

The more the attacks of doubt came, the more I prayed and read. Satan was indeed a formidable adversary, but I had God on my side regardless of what he wanted me to think. I knew from Revelations that Satan was the accuser of the believers, causing doubt and fear in the hearts of men. i also knew that it would be God's word that I would be proclaiming, and not my own. This knowledge helped to give me the calming assurance I needed to move forward.

I knew that I was finally free, no longer bound down by the weight of doubt and regret. I began to praise God. Tears of joy poured down my face as I rejoiced at the realization of the work God was doing inside of me. In that jail cell, I was finally free. I had made one of the greatest journeys of my life, from prison to praise.

As the next few weeks came and went, I felt stronger, and more confident, that what Paul had written in Romans 8:28 was real in my life.

> *"All things work together for good to them that love God, to them who are called according to His purpose."*

Each cell in the holding center had an intercom box which consisted of a call button, a speaker, and a microphone. This Intercom was so the officers could communicate with inmates, as needed, and they could be notified in the case of an emergency. The day finally came when, without warning or advance notice, a voice came through the speaker and directed me to prepare to leave. It was my day to go to court.

In all honesty, there was very little I could do to get ready. I had already been awake for some time, so I had already combed my hair and brushed my teeth before getting dressed. So basically all I had be, and wait for the officer to come and get me.

As I said, I was already awake when that pre-dawn call over the Intercom told me to get ready for court. This was my usual pattern carried over from when I was at home. I would always get up early enough so that I could spend about an hour every morning in prayer and personal Bible study to prepare myself spiritually for whatever might be in front of me that day. I liked starting my day with some intimate time with my Lord, putting Him first, before anything else that has to come.

That morning before court, I sat on my bunk reading from Hebrews, while waiting for the guards to open the door and take me to court. I read chapters eleven through thirteen, reminding myself that faith is the substance of things hoped for and the evidence of things not yet seen.

Verses five and six of the thirteenth chapter seemed to be written just for me that morning. It told me to be content with what I had, and God also promised, *"I will not leave thee or forsake thee."* What a promise from the creator and sustainer of all creation! I was ready. After all, *"The Lord is my helper and I shall not fear what man shall do unto me."*

I committed those two verses to memory, and I repeated them to myself over and over as I waited.

Finally, the door "clicked" open, and the guards started calling the names of everyone who was going to court that day. We were herded into a "sallyport," which is like a foyer with a door on either end. Once everyone was in the sallyport, the door separating us from the cell block was closed, locked, and secured. Once that was done, the door in front of us that lead out into the hallway clicked open.

We were walked to the front of the holding center to the booking area. Once we arrived, which took several minutes since we had to go through several locked doors to enter and exit different sections of the jail, we were all herded, once again, into a small room where we were told to wait. Not that we had much choice in the matter, but I guess it is policy for them to point out the obvious.

We waited in that room for close to an hour before the door finally opened. We all got up from where we were sitting, which was on a long, concrete bench which ran the length of the small cell we were in, but we were not going anywhere. When the door swung open, there was a guard along with one of the jail trustees standing there. "Breakfast," yelled the guard. Then the trustee started handing out paper bags to each of the inmates in the room.

After receiving our breakfast we all sat back down to eat. Let me stop here to say that calling this "breakfast" might be a little optimistic. What we had been given in these bags were, two pieces of wheat bread (soggy), one piece of bologna (green), one orange (also green), and a Styrofoam cup with a small packet of tropical punch-like Kool-Aid substitute (sugar-free). It was not much, but we all ate, not knowing when we would get to eat again.

About the time the last of us finished choking down our meal, the door opened and the trustee was standing there with a trash bag. "Trash," he yelled, and we all formed a line to walk by the door to throw our bags and cups away.

As soon as the trustee stepped away from the door, another officer was standing there. He said he wanted two of us to step out. This two at a time precession continued until everyone was brought out and prepared for transport.

We were all still dressed in our holding facility bright orange jumpsuits and rubber thonged sandals, or flip-flops as I had always called them. As we called out, two at a time, we were put in handcuffs and shackles, then we were put into the transport van. Eight of us were packed into a space only big enough for six people. Six very small people in my opinion.

After we were all loaded into the van, and the door was closed, locked, and secured, we had to sit there and wait for the drivers to finish their coffee and cigarettes before leaving. The whole time we were sitting there, most everyone kept saying things like, "I hope they hurry." After about the tenth time of hearing this I could not help but say, "Well, I hope no one passes gas." That little joke lightened the mood a little and got the rest of the guys joking around.

It was a forty mile journey to Florence, South Carolina, where we would all be making our appearance in front of the honorable judge who would be providing us with our federally mandated plans for the future. Even though we had at least two hours before we had to appear before the judge, the driver seemed to be in an awful big hurry. He was weaving in and out of traffic, and the speedometer showed that we were traveling at speeds that never dropped below 70 MPH, even though the signs clearly showed the posted speed limit to be 45 MPH.

When we hit the interstate, with a posted legal speed limit of 65 MPH, I could see the needle bouncing between 95 and 100 MPH the whole way to the courthouse. I was never so happy to pull into a parking garage as I was when we made it safely into that one. I would have got down on the ground and kissed the asphalt, if I did not think it would have gotten me into trouble with the transport officers. Some people just do not have a very good sense of humor, especially when it comes to their driving skills. Or lack thereof.

After we were safely parked, the transport officers unloaded us and crammed us into a small elevator. This was much more than simple herding, and brought to mind images of fat clowns and tiny cars. We went up a couple of floors then we were deposited into one of those famous federal government, all stainless steel holding cells/confinement areas. This is where we would wait for our turn in front of the judge. One up-side to it all was that the guards were kind enough to remove the handcuffs before they left. We just had to keep the shackles on. Hey, I'll take what I can get.

CHAPTER ELEVEN

I was still replaying those verses in my head when a court officer came in and called out a name. One by one, we were called out, taken in front of the judge, then brought back. Unlike before when someone went to see the judge and was never seen again; at least, not in the confinement area anyway.

As each person returned, he was placed in an adjoining holding cell where we could talk to one another; we just could not see one another. The tone of the conversation was not very encouraging, to say the least. The judge had given one fellow a sentence of 75 months, and another one got a sentence of 262 months. (The federal courts give sentences in months rather than years. I do not know why.)

There was a third individual who said the judge had given him 84 months for "ghost dope," and 60 more months tacked on top of that for a shotgun that was in a locked cabinet that belonged to his "Pops."

For those who do not know, "ghost dope" is dope the government *THINKS* you might have had. They do not have to have any proof at all. If they think it was at least possible that you could have gotten your hands on a particular amount of drugs then they go ahead and charge you with it.

At a little before noon, the Marshals came in and started handing out bag lunches to everyone. These were not great, but they were a lot better then what we were served for breakfast. Also, learning to balance on the edge of a stainless steel bench, unable to cross your legs thanks to the shackles, and removing and eating you government issued sandwiches was...engaging, to say the least. While we were also provided with paper cups to get water out of the toilet/sink combo to help wash the sandwiches down, we unfortunately were not given any Kool Aid-like powder in which to add to the water, so that the metallic taste of the water could be somewhat covered up.

After we ate, we waited. It seemed like we had to wait for hours until someone else was called out to see the judge. The longer I waited, the more I started to think that maybe, just maybe, God was going to miraculously move the judge to find me "not guilty" so that I could go home where I could work in my church to fulfill His calling for me.

What I did not know at the time was, with this kind of thinking,

I was seeking to serve God in a way that pleased ME. In a way, and place, that was comfortable to ME. I did not think it was unreasonable to want to be at home with my family where I could provide for them, and lead them spiritually. With MY plan, I would be back in my granddaughter's lives, to help shape and guide them as they grow. While this seemed like a good plan to me, there was still something that I was not taking into account. This plan, that was so well thought out by me, was "my will," and not "His will."

Many times I had thought up a plan and asked God to bless it. On some occasions, He would bless my plan; on other occasions, not so much. This plan would prove to be one of the latter.

Eventually I was called for. It was finally my time to see the judge, and I was actually looking forward to it this time. I was escorted back to another elevator, then taken to another floor in the building where I was lead down a long hallway before entering yet another elaborately decorated courtroom.

Upon entering the courtroom, I saw that my court appointed lawyer was already there, as was the prosecutor. The judge was not in the room yet, but the stenographer was there setting up her equipment so she could record everything that was said during the hearing. I guess that, even in these days of computer-everything, some things are still done the old fashioned way.

I shuffled over to the table where my lawyer had set up camp. Walking would not be an accurate description of how one must move in order to get from point "A" to point "B" while wearing leg shackles. Shackles which, for some reason, always seem to get heavier when I walk into a courtroom.

My lawyer and I greeted one another when I sat at the table. He said that we only had a few minutes to talk before the judge came in so he began explaining to me how the procedure would happen. I was informed that, once the judge came in and began with my case, I would stand before the judge with my lawyer at my side. During the hearing, I was to only answer questions with "yes, sir," or "No, sir." No other comments were expected or welcomed from me because the judge's ruling was already made, and nothing I could say was going to do anything to make the judge change his decision.

Once I was informed of how the hearing would go, my lawyer became engrossed in his paperwork until the judge came out for the hearing, which was only about ten minutes later. I felt a little like I was being ignored by my lawyer, to be honest. I mean, this was a pretty important day, and hearing, for me and I was nervous. A little conversation might have calmed my nerves a little. But I supposed he had other clients to worry about as much as he had to worry about me so, I did not bother him any more than necessary.

Finally, the judge made his way into the courtroom, along with a small crowd of other people, who I assume were clerks and whatnot. We all stood as a court officer called the court to order. Once the judge sat, I was lead to a podium by my lawyer. The podium sat a few feet forward of the prosecutors table to where I could not see him while looking at the judge. My lawyer stood off to my right, holding my file in his hands. It was quite thick. I do not know why I noticed that, but I did.

Standing at the podium, there was a microphone that I was instructed to speak into so that everything I said could be recorded, and so the Judge could hear me as well. The podium stood at least fifty feet from where the judge was so he would have had trouble hearing me had I not been speaking into the microphone. The room truly was immense.

The charges against me were read. As the judge read the charges, he would on occasion peer at me over the tops of his reading glasses, disapproval radiated from the man. After the charges were read, the judge asked the prosecutor about "relevant conduct." Relevant conduct is what the prosecution Believes they could prove if the case went to trial.

It is what the court expects the defendant to admit to and plead guilty to, even if what the prosecution "believes" happened, really did or not.

In federal court, I was learning, actual guilt or innocence makes little difference. It is all about getting someone to plead guilty so that the prosecutor's office can keep their 90+% conviction rate.

As the prosecutor read the relevant conduct, which the judge had in front of him anyway, he also read a couple of statements from other people who were involved in the conspiracy that I was being charged with being a part of. I kind of expected one or two of the people to give statements against me but, what amazed me most was, there was even a statement from someone I had never even met before, and his statement made it sound like we had been the best of friends for years. I could not believe what I was hearing.

During the whole hearing, my lawyer did what he said he would do. He stood right beside me. The problem was, that is all he did. Not one time did he speak out to challenge anything the prosecution was saying.

If I looked his way in the hope of getting him to say something, he would suddenly find southing very interesting to look at on his shirt sleeve or in my file he was holding. It was very frustrating, but there was nothing I could say or do about it so, I just stood there quietly, like I was told to do, while all these extremely negative statements were read against me.

After what seemed like forever, the prosecutor stopped talking and the judge looked towards my lawyer, who did not have anything to say.

No argument of any kind over the statements that were made against me or anything. He just stood there. So, the judge looks at me, looks at my file and flips through it a little, then looks at me again. He asks if i have anything to say. I was not expecting this so, now that I am being given the chance to speak, I figured I had better take it. I told the judge a little about my history, and about how God has moved me to speak for Him. I explained how I had been working hard to minister to the men coming into the jail, and how I felt like God had a mission for me. i admitted that I had come, short of God's glory a few times, and that I was truly sorry for that. I poured my heart out to this judge, and I begged for his mercy.

Unfortunately, mercy was not the order of the day for my judge. After I had finished talking, he told me that he was sorry to hear I had slipped away from the church the way I had and gotten myself in so much trouble.

He also told me that he honestly hoped I was serious about the mission I felt like God had set before me, I assured him that I was.

Then the judge started telling me that nearly all of the defendants who come before him had suddenly "found God." They would write him letter after letter, swearing that now that they had God in their lives, they would never commit a crime again. There had even been a couple of times, he explained, where inmates have taken correspondence course through the mail, to become ordained ministers. I was beginning to think that this judge did not know whether someone came before him professing their love for the Lord was serious from jailhouse religion. So, in order to be on the safe-side, he just assumed everyone was lying.

I told the judge that I was very serious in my love for God, and the work He has given me. I told him I was not one of these guys who just used God as a way to try to get out of jail, and that my history with the church BEFORE my arrest should be enough to prove that. The judge just smiled at me and said he was very happy to hear that I was serious because he was going to help me in my work for the Lord. His help, he told me, would be in supplying me with a very captive audience. Then he sentenced me to 120 months in prison.

As soon as he had sentenced me, the judge walked back out of the courtroom. I was lead to a table where I had to sign some papers that my lawyer had for me. I asked him why he had not said anything to try to help me. He told me that his job was to get me through sentencing, with as little damage as possible, and that was it. His job was finished.

CHAPTER TWELVE

I was in a state of shock the day I left the courtroom, after being sentenced. When all of this started, my lawyer told me I was looking at 42-60 months. That was bad enough. Then, when it came time to sign my plea agreement, the minimum the prosecution was asking for was 188 months. When the Judge sentenced me to the 120 months, the first thing I felt was sick to my stomach. I felt, for a minute, like God had decided to abandon me at the last minute. That way of thinking did not last long. As soon as I caught my mind moving in that direction I reminded myself that, while I DID get 5 years more than I first expected, I also got 5 years LESS than the prosecutor had been asking for. I felt the hand of God working there so I took as much comfort in that knowledge as I was able to.

No, God had not rescued me, like I thought He was going to, but I still felt like He had more in store for me, and for my future so I resolved to wait and see what happened next. I would keep my trust in God, and I would accept whatever it was He wanted me to do. No matter what it was, or how long it took.

Now that I was sentenced, it was time to start my journey towards whatever prison I would be going to in order to serve my sentence. The first stop on my journey was at a jail in Effingham, which is near Florence, SC. There were several of us on that trip, and after we arrived, we were all placed in a large holding cell, where we waited, after our cuffs and shackled were removed

By the time we were all booked in, strip searched, finger printed, and whatnot, it was close to eleven o'clock at night. Finally, we were moved to a cell block where we could get some sleep. Which I did as soon as my head laid down on the blanket they had given me, which I used for a pillow.

No sooner had I fallen asleep, it seemed like, someone was waking me up and telling me to pack it up again. I was leaving. I got up and brushed my teeth and washed my face before gathering up my blanket and waiting to be taken to wherever it was I was going to this time. As I was being lead back down the hallway towards booking again, I looked at a clock we were passing and it read 3:00am, maybe a little after.

I had been to sleep for less than four hours.

I was seated on a bench with four other guys. Directly in front of us was a holding cell with a large window that was facing us. Inside the cell were a couple females who were also waiting to be transported. A couple of the guys started talking to the girls, and it was not long before the talk became somewhat... suggestive.

Within a matter of minutes, the girls started putting on a show for the guys. It started out with a little flirting and teasing but soon turned into something more, with each of the girls trying to out-do the other.

From their protective position behind the glass, the girls became more and more emboldened. They started taking off, and pulling down, what little clothing they had on, and the more they took off, the more noise the guys made. As you can imagine, it did not take long before all of the noise attracted the attention of the booking officers. When one of the female officers came around the corner to see what the noise was about, and saw what was taking place, we were immediately moved to another area, out of sight of the females, but not so far away that we could not hear the officer sharply addressing the issue with the girls.

One by one, we were strip searched, shackled, chained, and cuffed before being loaded into a transport van. Two men were loaded into the middle seat and three men were loaded into the back seat. The front seat, directly behind the drivers, was reserved for two female passengers.

These were not the same females who were putting on the show in the booking area. Apparently, according to one of the drivers, those particular women had been arrested at a local strip-club, and they were being charged with prostitution and possession of drugs. They were just waiting for transport to court, not transfer like we were.

When we pulled out of the sallyport at the jail, it was still pre-dawn. Everyone was tired and probably a little nervous since none of us knew where we were going this time. One of the guys started talking to the girls, but this time the conversation was a little more normal, and respectful. He just asked things like their names, where they were from, how much time they had, what their charges were, and things of that nature. He even started asking if they were in relationships with anyone. That is something else about people who are locked up, and who are going to be locked up for a long time. They will often "hook up," meaning they will write one another during their incarcerations as if they are boyfriend/girlfriend, and often they have never even met before.

It is an illusion, and everyone knows it, but they will make plans and whatnot, even knowing that those plans will never happen. It is an easy way to combat loneliness.

Heading down the interstate, I just assumed that we were going to Atlanta, Georgia. The prison there is a transfer center for inmates who are coming into the system for the first time, and for inmates who are transferring from one prison to another. By the time the morning sun was high in the sky, I figured out that Atlanta was not going to be our destination.

Seeing as I had made many trips up and down I-95 as a truck driver, I pretty much knew every turnoff we went by. I also knew we were heading towards Jesup, Ga. when we took the Richmond Hill exit because I had lived in Jesup for a while several years before. What confused me was that, while I knew that there was a federal prison in Jesup, I had no idea that they housed new inmates there while waiting to be designated.

I especially could not figure out what they were planning on doing with the females since the prison there was males only.

There was no need to worry. We did not go to Jesup. Instead, we arrived at another facility that was basically way out in the middle of nowhere in Ocilla, Georgia, and this would be "home" for a while.

In the federal system, after a person is arrested, charged, and finally convicted and sentenced, the person does not go directly to prison- He is usually sent to a holding facility until he is designated to the facility where he will do his time. This can take several months, and the person can be bounced around from holding facility to holding facility before finally arriving at his designation.

After arriving<at Ocilla, we went through the whole booking-in process, then we were issued clothing, sheets, blankets, and a hygiene kit which consisted of soap/ tooth brush, and tooth paste, and a comb. Finally we were taken, as a group, to where the cells/dorms were located. I was taken to the old part of the jail where there were nothing but open dorms. There were a lot of people in the open dorms and it was pretty noisy.

That, however, did not keep me from laying down and getting a good, long nights sleep.

Early the next morning, I was awakened for breakfast. I got in line with everyone else, and then we were walked, single file with our hands behind our back and right shoulder next to the wall, to the chow hall.

There was a guard at the door to the unit directing us out into the hall, another guard in the hall directing us to the chow hall, and still another guard standing at the chow hall door directing us inside. We filed through the door, picked up a tray, and went to the table, all while staying in the same order. There was no sitting beside your buddy or home boy or whatever. Everyone sat down together, beside whoever was in front and behind you in line. We were not allowed to speak in the hallway on our way to or from chow, and we were not allowed to speak in the chow hall either. If you started to talk, the officer working the chow hall would assume you were finished eating, and he would take your tray and throw the food away. Needless to say, it was best to keep your mouth shut unless you were putting a spoon in it.

We were given about five minutes to eat. About the time the last of the line was coming through the door; those who were first were told to leave. They would get up and drop their trays off as they filed out another door, back into the hallway.

Depending on how much staff was on duty, sometimes each table would be walked on back to the unit right then, but other times they would have to wait, quietly, in the hall until everyone had finished. Then everyone would be walked the fifty or so feet back to the unit.

You did NOT bring food back to the unit from the chow hall. Not ever, and for no reason. There were a few guys who were diabetic, and they got to bring a snack bag back if it was part of their APPROVED diet plan, but other than that, you had better not get caught trying to sneak food back unless you wanted to go to the "hole." The guards made sure to repeat this rule to us several times on our way to chow, and while we were eating.

Once I made it back from breakfast, I felt a little more alert since I had had a good night's rest and some food. I decided to spend a little time looking around and getting to know my surroundings. There were two floors in the unit. The upper floor was more loft-like, and they looked down onto the first floor. On the second floor, there were about fifty beds, twenty-five sets of bunk beds. There was also a small bathroom that was open to the entire unit. This bathroom consisted of two sinks and two toilets.

On the first floor, there was a booth that was entirely enclosed by tinted glass. When they were actually there, this is where the guards would sit. There was a shelf along one wall which contained two microwaves for inmate use. Along another wall were several telephones.

Just like on the second floor, there was a small, open bathroom. Beside this bathroom was a large shower area. The area was surrounded on three sides by block walls and the front was covered with a large shower curtain of sorts, inside the shower, there were several shower heads so that ten or more people could shower at the same time. There were no partitions or divisions between shower heads.

The shower area, I was to learn later, was appropriately called the "Thunder Dome." Anytime anyone had a dispute with someone else, the parties involved would go into the shower to settle it. This was the only area in the unit that was out of sight of the officers.

Most of the people In the unit had went back to bed after breakfast. There were a few guys still up so I started talking to some of them to find out what was what at that facility. I was filled in on the three gangs that were in our unit, and how they did not get along very well.

It was commonly believed that the officers chose not to separate the gangs because they enjoyed watching the action that popped off quite often.

I did not like the thought of being in such a violent environment so I went back to my bed and prayed for God to protect me while I was there and I asked Him for guidance in knowing who I should and should not talk to, or hang around with. I also asked if there was anyone I should try speaking to about Him, and if so I asked to be lead to that person, or persons.

Lunch was pretty much just a repeat of breakfast, as far as the parade to the chow hall and back. There was one exception however. On the way to the chow hall, someone at the front of the line called attention to a glass door to our right. As we passed by, I glanced that way, following the gaze of the guys in front of me. It was a gym, and it was full of females.

The girls did not notice us as we walked by but the guys sure noticed them. They started slow-walking the door in an attempt to see every girl in the gym, and there were a lot of them. Some were standing, some were sitting. Some were playing basketball, and some were just walking around the outer edge of the room.

The officers noticed the slow down and one of them barked out, "get stepping," as they called it. By the time we left the chow hall, someone had taped a big piece of cardboard over window of the gym door. You might think I am kidding about this but there were actually guys who were walking slow and staring at the cardboard like they really thought they would suddenly be able to see through it. I do not know what goes through some people's minds sometimes.

With lunch over, people were beginning to stir around a little more. Some of the guys were walking and some were exercising by doing pushups and sit-ups. Some were doing pull-ups and others were even using the bunk beds as makeshift bench presses. There were a lot of little groups of people around, engrossed in whatever conversations they were having. Basically, everyone doing his own thing.

I walked by a table where three guys, I will call them Bill, Bob, and Nate, were sitting with open Bibles, and deep into a discussion.

I paused to see what the subject matter was and introduced myself. After everyone had introduced himself, I was invited to join in on their talk. I accepted their invitation and sat down.

They were discussing the meaning of salvation that day. One of the guys said that he wanted the assurance of Heaven, but he was not sure he could be "good enough" to get there. This was Bill. Bob told him that what he needed to do was to pray, and ask God to help him clean up his act. That is actually good advice for anyone, in my opinion. Nate, on the other hand, told him that as long as he believed that there was a Jesus then he would be alright. Nate supported his position by saying that that is what he had done. Nate when the preacher prayed with him, and he said that he believed in Jesus, he got this feeling inside that he would never forget.

Bob finally invited me into the conversation by asking what my thoughts were on the subject. I asked all three of the guys how much of their Bibles they had read. All three books look pretty new to me. Bob said that he had read a little of it "here and there," but that was about it. Bill said all that he had read was a little in Proverbs and Psalms, along with a little of the New Testament. Nate said he could not really understand what he was reading, but he said he still tried to read a couple verses every day.

CHAPTER THIRTEEN

I felt like it was meant for me to meet, and talk with, Bill, Bob, and Nate. Here were three men who had really had much in the way of religious upbringings and yet they were trying, on their own, to learn about God. This was a true desire to learn also, not just a case, or cases, of jailhouse religion. I also felt that there was a lot these men could learn from me, and maybe there would even be something I could learn from them.

In answer to their questions about salvation, and if they could be forgiven and accepted into the Kingdom of Heaven, I borrowed Bob's Bible and opened it to Genesis. With the rest of the guys following along in the other Bibles, I began reading about how God had SPOKEN everything into existence. "Think about that for a minute," I told them. "With a word, God created the earth, the light, the water, plants and animals. He also created man from the dust of the earth and breathed the breath of life into him so that he became a living soul."

I explained to them that God had created mankind in order to have a relationship with them. I told them that God would speak to man, just like we were speaking to one another right there, at that moment. God loved mankind, and He gave them the earth, and the power to rule over all the creatures of the earth.

God only had one rule that he expected man to follow; but man violated that rule by eating from the tree of forbidden fruit. By doing so, man's eyes were opened, and he saw that he was naked before God, and he was ashamed. He made a covering for himself with fig leaves and tried bidding from God, but God called him out.

God told man that the results of his sin could not be covered by leaves, only blood could do that so, God killed an animal and gave the skin to man to use as a covering. I have no proof of this but I personally believe that the animal was a lamb because, John speaking of Jesus said, "Behold, the Lamb of God that takes away the sins of the world." Scripture also states that without the shedding of blood, there is no remission of sin.

I took the group to Paul's writings in the book of Romans, 3:23, and showed them,

> *"All have sinned and come short of the glory of God."*

I explained that, there is no one on this earth who is "good enough, all the time. Everyone had disappointed God in some way, at some time, in his life. The trick was to repent from those sins, and to ask forgiveness for them.

I explained to them that God is righteous and holy, and He could not let sin go unpunished. We turned to Romans 6:23 where we read, *"The wages of sin is death but the gift of God is eternal life through Jesus Christ, our Lord."* only through

Jesus Christ, and the blood He shed, could we be saved and allowed to enter Heaven. And, all we had to do to accept this gift from God was to ask for it. No matter what we had done, we could be forgiven.

The guys in the group had a lot of questions about what we had just read, and I was more than happy to help them learn. None of them had ever had the Bible explained to them, at least not like I was taking the time to do it, and they wanted to know more.

Bill asked me if I would care to meet with them daily and maybe even privately, to study more and to help them understand better what they were reading. I said that I would be happy to help them but I needed to get myself a Bible. Nate left the table but returned a few minutes later with a new paperback Bible he had gotten from somewhere.

That evening, we went through the same routine for dinner.

Afterward, it was our turn to go to the gym. We got to play basketball, walk or run around the court, and do some exercising or whatever we felt like doing. When we came back to the unit, my three new friends asked me if I would like to join them again to tell them more about what we had discussed earlier. I was more than happy to share whatever I could with them so, I went and got my new Bible then met them at the table we had used earlier that day.

Knowing that none of these guys had a very good understanding of the Bible, I told them that before they began reading, whether alone or as a group, they should always start out with a prayer- I told them that God would not put his word in front of them and not have them be able to understand what it was He was trying to tell them. "Pray to God,"

I said to them, "And ask Him to open your minds and hearts so that you can receive His word." With that being said, I lead the group in a prayer, asking God to do just that very thing for us.

Nate still had questions about salvation. He asked me to go back to what we had talked about earlier and explain to them, from the Bible, what one should do when he realizes he is a sinner. He asked what he had to do to pay for his sins.

John 3:16, the Bible's most well to passage, says,

> *"For God so loved the world that He gave His only begotten Son, that whosoever believeth in Him shall not perish, but have everlasting life."*

I told the guys that WE could not pay our sin debt. That is why Jesus came. He died to pay our debt for us. I told them that Acts 20:21 says we must have repentance toward God and faith in Jesus Christ. That is how we gain salvation. God made a way for us to be saved when He gave His Son, and it was up to us to place our faith in him.

The Bible saying we have to believe goes much deeper than just saying that God sent Jesus here for the purpose of dying for our sins. The "believing" that is being spoken of is a total commitment by surrendering to do the will of God. This is faith that we accept the finished work of Jesus on the cross to be the payment for our personal sin debt, and repent, which means that we turn away from a life that is self-centered. Choosing instead to live out a life that is pleasing to God, according to what scripture teaches us.

Wanting to know if what I was reading and explaining to these guys was really getting through to them, I asked them if they thought they would be allowed to enter Heaven if they had to stand before God right this very minute? Would God say to you, "Well done my good and faithful servant?" Or, would he say, "Depart from me you worker of iniquity, I never knew you?"

Although I had directed the question to all of them, I turned to Bill first for an answer. He said that he thought he would be alright he had joined a church when he was younger, although he did not go that often.

Bob said that he did believe he had broke the ten commandments bad enough that he would not be allowed in, and besides that, he felt like he was a pretty good person. They both said that maybe they would not have gotten in if they had to stand before God a few months ago, maybe even a few weeks ago, but now that they were being serious about trying to worship God, they thought that tipped the scales a little more in their favor. I knew I was going to have my hands full with these two.

I saved Nate for last because I could just feel that he was taking in everything I was telling him. When I posed the same question to him, Nate said that he honestly did not believe he would make it in if he had to stand before God on that day. But, he also said that he wanted that fact to change. Immediately.

We spoke for a long time that evening. Finally, I ask Nate if he was ready to receive Christ by faith and repent now. He said that he was, and that night, I had the privilege of leading him in a prayer of repentance and confession, where he asked Jesus into his heart. After we finished praying, Nate said that he truly felt as if the weight of the world had been lifted off of him.

Bill spoke up and said that he too had prayed that prayer with us, and he said he also felt the presence of God within him, making him feel as if he were all new inside like he had never felt before. This time, he told me, he was sure that there had been a change inside him because, when he prayed that prayer, that is what he wanted more than anything he had ever wanted before in his life.

Suddenly, our celebration was interrupted by a disturbance in the unit. There was the sound of someone screaming and cussing, and there was the voice of one of the Mexicans, who was shouting something in Spanish.

We jumped up from our table and ran in the direction of the noise. By the time we got to where we were able to see, which was halfway up the stairs so we could see over top of everyone else who was gathering around, the area around the disturbance had cleared out. This left the person who was doing all the screaming alone in the middle of the floor.

We saw a large, muscular black man trying to remove his t-shirt. Once he got it off, we saw the cause of his anguish. The skin on his chest, abdomen, and half his face had been literally melted away. From what we were being told, the Mexican kid had taken a cup of baby oil and boiled it in the microwave. Then he threw if in the black man's face.

Within minutes, the door to the unit flew open and the jail's special squad of guards, call ICE, came rushing in, dressed all in black, pointing Tasers, and shouting orders for everyone to get down on the floor. They made their way to the center of the action. Two of the guards grabbed the injured man while several more grabbed the Mexican, who the unit officer had pointed out to them as being the one who had committed the atrocious act.

The guards surrounded him, subdued him, and then roughly removed him from the unit, after cuffing him securely. Only the inmates involved had been removed from the unit, we were all directed to go to our bunks until further notice. Four of the ICE team stayed in the unit to make sure that everyone did in fact return to their bunks, and to make sure order was restored.

All of the Mexican guys lived in the same area, which was located in one corner of the lower floor. Once everyone had returned to their bunks, and gotten settled down, the rest of the Mexicans were told to roll up their gear. The ICE team escorted them out of the unit once they had packed up.

It took a while for everything to get back to normal but eventually we were permitted to leave our beds again, and to resume all normal operations, as they say. Once we were our table, the guys in the group began to fill me in a little on what they knew about what had been going on in the unit, and that had lead up to the evening's horrific events.

I was informed that the black man was a member of the Bloods street gang. The Mexican was a member of the well known, and extremely ruthless, MS-13 street gang. Apparently, the two factions had been "beefing," which means that there had been some kind of trouble brewing between the two gangs for some time now. From what I was able to determine, if I understood everything correctly, was that the so-called beef was over which of the two gangs was going to be the dominate force in the unit.

Who was most powerful, and who was going to gain control of that imaginary title. I know that it seems obvious to most of us that this quest is ridiculous anywhere. But the simple fact that Ocilla was nothing more than a temporary holdover facility made it all seem even more juvenile.

Spiritually, because of the work done by Jesus Christ, and the sacrifice he made, the Holy Spirit has established ownership inside of all of us. The enemy of mankind, however, is Satan, who seeks to steal, kill, and destroy. While the Holy Spirit was bringing Nate and Bill to a relationship with Jesus, Satan was hard at work causing hatred and bodily harm between two other men.

Bob posed a question that many of us are forced to find our own answer to; "How can a loving God allow such a terrible thing to happen?"

I told Bob that God had once created man to be perfect, and He had also given him a perfect environment in which to live- the Garden of Eden. Then, I told him about how Satan had once led a rebellion against God, because of his own jealousy and pride. For some reason, Satan felt like he should have been greater than God, who had actually created him as Lucifer, the most beautiful of all God's angels.

Lucifer was not alone in his rebellion against God, but he and his followers were eventually defeated and cast down from Heaven. Since he could not de-throne God, he began to attack God's most prized creation—man.

I explained to Bob that God gave us a choice after Satan had tempted Eve, and by doing so, brought sin into the hearts of mankind. He wants to have a relationship with us, but it has to be our choice. He will not force us because He did not create us to be like robots.

By having a choice, some people choose to exercise that freewill to do harm to others. They want to inflict pain and agony. That is the power Satan has over us, and it is up to us to ask God to help us fight against that power. Or, we can give in to it, be lead around by the nose by Satan disobeying God, and then paying the consequences for our choices.

It was very obvious that Bob was tormented over a lot of things. Aside from the obvious, such as being incarcerated and taken away from his family and friends, he was also struggling with the things he thought were true, but he was finding out were... less than true. He thought he had lived a good life, and he was finding out that there was more to living for God than giving to the local food drive on occasion.

Bob was also struggling with what he should and should not believe.

He was starting to look at things differently now that he had someone who was willing to take the time to explain it all to him. Just as I had gotten to pray with Bill and Nate earlier, I also prayed with Bob that night as he accepted Christ as his personal Lord and Savior. All in all, it was a wonderful day for Jesus.

As I went to bed that night, I could not help but to praise God for allowing me the opportunity to be a part of His team. To see the joy and peace those three guys had was simply priceless to me. I also prayed for the two men who were involved in the altercation earlier in the evening. I prayed that God would bring healing into both of their lives; both physically and spiritually, and I prayed that their eyes would be opened so that they would be able to see' and understand where their lives were headed if they did not make a change, and soon.

CHAPTER FOURTEEN

Our little group continued to meet two and three times a day. We would be joined occasionally by someone new who was just coming in, or by someone who was leaving, and who wanted us to pray for them. No one was ever turned away, even if we thought they had joined us simply to ask crazy questions of us in order to try to mock us or the Lord, which happened from time to time. When this did happen, we would answer the questions to the best of our abilities, and I always hoped that by doing so we had planted a seed that would eventually lead the person to Christ.

While we were in our little group, there was always a lot going on around us. You had guys playing chess, guys playing checkers. There were a lot of card games going on; poker, spades, hearts. There were even guys in the unit who were doing tattoo work.

T. M. Rain and Michael Hall

Tattoos are very common in jails, prisons, and detention centers, people get them for a number of different reasons. Some people will get the names of their children, wife, or parents. Some will get work done that shows their affiliation with a certain gang. Still others will get religious based tattoos.

Boredom is one of the reasons for getting tattooed in jail. There just is not a lot to do so people have to find things to keep them busy. Some people start missing their family and they get the names of those closest to them tattooed on because it makes the inmate feel closer to those they .1.., or to pay tribute to a loved one who has passed away Sometimes the person who passed away is a parent or a grandparent.

On a lot of occasions, people will get religious based work done simply because they feel it will give them while incarcerated, or that God will be so flattered that He will help the person get out of jail sooner. There are those who get religious work done because they sincerely do love God, but, unfortunately (from my experience anyway), those people are the minority.

Some of the tattoo artists are very good at what they do, and sometimes the motivation for getting tattooed in jail is cost. Jailhouse tattoo work is very cheap. Someone can get, and I have seen this myself over the years, several thousands of dollars worth of work done for a couple hundred dollars. For most jailhouse tattoo artists, there art is their only source of income.

Getting tattooed in jail or prison is not exactly safe, and it is definitely against the rules. Tattoo guns are made by removing the motors from hair or beard trimmers. The rest of the tattoo machine is made from other things like the tube and tip of an ink pen, along with a few other misc. parts and pieces. The needles are often made from guitar strings, the springs out of ink pens, or staples.

Ink is made a few different ways, but mostly it involves burning something like baby oil, plastic cups, checkers, chess pieces, or just about anything else that smokes heavily with black smoke so that the smoke can be captured in a bag or on the bottom of a soda can. The soot from the burning material is then mixed with water, or sometimes shampoo (or a combination or the two), and the ink is ready for use.

Despite the crude method of making the tattooing machines and ink, there are people who do some beautiful work. The first tattoo I ever saw given in this manner was done by a Mexican in Ocilla. The tattoo he was doing on another Mexican was praying hands with the guy's mother's name under them. The Mexican was using a staple out of a magazine that had been sharpened by rubbing it on the concrete floor. Once the staple was sharp, it was inserted into the eraser of a pencil, then a little thread, which was pulled out of a shirt, was wrapped around the staple. This was done so that the thread could hold ink while the tattoo was being applied. I was shocked at the quality of work this guy was able to do in this primitive manner. The work, once it had healed, looked as if it had been done by a professional in an actual tattoo parlor.

Not all pursuits are quite so artistic when you have a hundred or more men crammed into such a confined living area, with boredom, worry, stress, and no outlet for building frustrations, little things can turn into serious situations very quickly.

One night, two gang members, from different gangs (one black, the other white), headed into the shower to settle a sudden dispute. The fight did not last all that long, but it was long enough for quite a bit of damage to get done.

Although the guards could not see inside the shower to know what was going on, it was normally pretty obvious that there was a fight going on in the shower are, whenever one broke out. The reason for this is that, whenever there was a fight going on, there would be representatives from the gangs of each person fighting standing in groups in front of the shower while the fight happened. If the person fighting did not belong to a particular gang, there would be representatives from the person's race standing around. This was to ensure the fight was fair. Also, when there was a fight, it got very quiet in the unit. Everyone would be trying to hear what was going on in the shower area.

On this night, it was only a few minutes before the guard realized that something was going on, and he was able to call the ICE team in to break it up. Once the fight was broken up, the black gang member had gotten the better of the white gang member.

The black guy was bleeding from his mouth and nose, and one

eye was swollen pretty bad, but the white guy could not even walk out of the shower, having suffered, among other injuries, a broken leg and a few broken ribs. He was bleeding so badly that you could not even see what color his hair was.

Both men were removed from the unit, and taken for medical attention. We found out later that the fight was over nothing more than a friendly game of cards. Apparently, one of the guys accused the other of cheating. An argument started then escalated pretty quickly to the point of name calling and racial slurs. Finally, the challenge was issued, "Let's take it to 'Thunder Dome." Male pride, and testosterone being the forces most see as the cause of the altercation, I believe God looks at it just like He did with Cain and Able. It is sin in the heart of man who seeks to harm or kill another man who was created in the image of God.

On the morning of my birthday, at around 4am, I was

awakened and told to pack out. I was leaving Ocilla, it would seem. I got up and looked around. A few others were getting up as well and getting ready to go.

Once we were ready, we were escorted to a holding cell in booking to wait out-processing.

Sometime around 6am or so, we were cuffed, shackled, chained, then packed into yet another transport van for another leg of our journey.

I remember thinking that we must be running late because the transport officer who was driving was flooring it every time he took off from a stop. He was slinging us around in the back of the van every time he went around a curve, and throwing us forward every time he had to make another stop. The ride was so rough that one of the guys in the back seat got sick to his stomach and threw up.

Once we got to the interstate, the ride smoothed out a little. The temperature, however, was beginning to rise inside the van, and the odor along with it. Since there was a partition made of Plexiglas that separated the inmates section from the drivers, the officers did not seem in the least bit bothered by the heat, or the smell. They were in a world of their own. For all intents and purposes, you would have thought that they did not even know that we were back there.

We made it to Atlanta and took an exit that was marked "Airport.

After a few more twists and turns, we pulled into an out-of-the-way back entrance near some buildings. We were allowed out of the van in order to used the restroom, then we were locked back in with no A/C or ventilation. We sat there for what felt like several hours while the officers stood outside smoking, drinking cold sodas, and joking around.

Finally, the officers got back into the van and drove us to

another area where there were other vans, cars, and buses waiting. There was a large, white airplane sitting on the tarmac. This was the all-too-famous Con-Air.

All around the plane stood heavily armed men and women. Inmates of every race, sex, age, size, and color were being loaded and unloaded from the plane, vans, cars, and buses'. I do not know how they kept track of who was going where, but they did. In fact, there was one group in a van who had to go back to where they came from because the officers forgot to bring their paperwork.

We got our chance to join the fray and were loaded onto the plane after being thoroughly searched. Once on the plane, we were instructed were to sit, and we were told to fasten our seat belts. A real pain when you are cuffed and those cuffs are locked onto a chain around your waist. There were people who had it even worse than most of us. Those guys were "black boxed." When you are black boxed, the officers put this black metal box thing over the cuffs themselves. This black box restricts the movement of your hands even more than just having the cuffs on. Black boxes are used on people with a history of violence, assault on officers or other inmates, and sometimes they are used for disciplinary reasons.

After everyone was loaded onto the plane, we took off. After we reached our cruising altitude, the inmates were allowed to go to the restroom, two at a time. Given the seriousness of the job, you would think the transport officers would have been a little more professional than what they were. There were maybe eight of them, and they spent the entire flight bantering back and forth with sexual comments towards one another, and talking about their personal lives. I found their behavior to be very unprofessional.

From the seat I was sitting in, I had a direct view of the galley.

At one point during the flight, two of the female transport officers were talking about serving lunch. One of the officers said, "I really don't feel like dealing with it today." With that said, the two officers started throwing the pre-packaged lunch meals into the trash receptacle.

We did not get any lunch that day.

Flying over those clouds that day made me start to think about the day when I would get to go to heaven. Having never flown over clouds in the day time before, I was seeing the tops of the clouds with the sun bouncing off of them, and it was beautiful. I began to think about spending an eternity with God, and being able to one day walk on those clouds. I stayed immersed in those thoughts until we began to descend, and everything disappeared.

We touched down at almost the same instant we broke through the cloud cover. It seemed like the same instant type anyway.

From Prison to Praise

Once we were on the ground, the plane taxied for what must have been at least two miles to a separate area of the airport. There, we parked at an uploading ramp that lead into a huge building that was several stories tall.

Just as I was about to step out of the enclosed ramp, the guy behind me accidentally stepped on the chain to my shackles, which caused me to nearly fall down. This earned me a stern reprimand by one of the guards to "stop playing around."

We entered a very long corridor where we played follow the leader until we came upon several benches along both sides of the corridor.

We were told to sit, which we all did without argument or delay. Despite what you might think or have seen on television, it hurts to walk or stand with leg shackles on. The metal cuts right into your legs, and even though you may be wearing socks, there is really not enough padding to make the experience much more comfortable.

Five at a time, we were told to stand on this platform where officers removed our chains, cuffs, and shackles. They were very efficient at doing this and had us all run through in no time at all. After everyone was unchained and whatnot, we were all lead into another area where we were told to undress. Once naked, we were sent through an "inspection area" where a guard with a flashlight sat on a stool, repeating the same orders to each inmate as we were marched through; "Bend over. Spread 'em. Next." I guess they were looking for contraband or weapons. No matter what they were looking for, that had to be the worst job of all.

After that humiliation, we were each given a pair of boxers, a pair of pants and t-shirt, and a pair of sandals. Then we were permitted to get dressed. Once dressed, we were directed to an area marked by divisions of the alphabet corresponding to the first letter of our last name. It was funny to me (and maybe it should not have been) that this step must have been just a little bit too complicated because there were actually people asking where they were supposed to go.

Each line led to an officer sitting at a long desk. When it was my turn to step up to the desk, I gave the officer my name. She checked it off a list then gave me a clipboard with a questionnaire on it, and told me to fill it out, which I did. Once filled out, I returned the clip board and questionnaire to the same woman who remarked about it being my birthday. She then said she was going to give me, "A little present." As you can imagine, that comment made me a little nervous.

There were several large cells where people were being sent to once they had finished filling out their questionnaires. I went to my assigned cell and waited with the others who were already there. In small groups, we were eventually brought out to yet another area where we were issued our bedding. While I was there, the lady officer walked around the corner, saw me standing there, and approached me. She handed me a brown paper bag, and instructed me to put it in my blanket and wait until I got to my room to open it.

As our names were called, we got in little groups and followed an officer to the elevator. I was taken to the sixth floor before being taken to the unit I was assigned to. My room was at the end of a hallway, near the showers.

The room I was assigned to already had one occupant when I got there. This was a rather dark-skinned Hispanic man. I had been given a medical bottom bunk pass so I was supposed to get the bottom bunk. Unfortunately, the room's other occupant already had his stuff on that bed. Not wanting to cause and ripples, I started to put my stuff on the top bunk.

My new roommate woke up and saw me for the first time. He

smiled and sat up, introducing himself as "Mr. Willy." Mr. Willy got up off the bed and told me to hold on while he moved his stuff. He said that he did not know how long it would be until they gave him a roommate so he was using the bottom bunk until then. "No reason to let it go to waste," he told me in his broken English. I could see, and agree with, his point.

T. M. Rain and Michael Hall

CHAPTER FIFTEEN

Once I had my bed made, and got a long awaited shower, I sat down to open the paper bag the lady officer had given me. Insdie the bag was a treasure consisting of coffee packets, creamers, sweeteners, four individually wrapped pieces of yellow cake, and a gospel tract. My new roommate and I celebrated my birthday together with coffee and cake. Afterwards, I laid down and did not move until the next morning.

The next morning, Mr. Willy woke, breakfast. After we ate, he showed me around, and tried to explain to me in the best english he could, how things worked around there, such as meals, laundry, count times, ect... He showed me the TV rooms, and where the phones were located and where I could go to find books, if I wanted to read, and he explained to me about the orderly who would come around with the hygiene cart.

The hygiene cart was just that; a cart. On it were individual packets of soap, shampoo, lotion, toothpaste, razors, toothbrushes, and combs.

We would be given what we needed to get us through the week. If you ran out, you could go ask the unit CO (correctional officer) for more, but that was often as much fun as having teeth pulled so most people made what they were given last until the next time the orderly came around.

Mr. Willy was a very nice guy, and he was very religious. He had a Bible that was written in Spanish, and he would spend about an hour a day reading it. I found a Bible for myself and spent most of my time reading and studying it. There were no regular prayer groups in my unit, and unfortunately there were no inmates interested in getting one started, I had just started to get settled in at this transfer center, which by the way was in

From Prison to Praise

Oklahoma City, Oklahoma, when I was called to the front and told to prepare to leave. I had been designated and had to catch Con-Air once again.

At the time of my sentencing, the judge asked if there was somewhere particular I wanted to go to do my time. This is standard in the federal court system. If you ask, the judge will make what is called a judicial recommendation that you be allowed to go to a particular prison to serve your time. Most people ask to go to certain places because of educational reasons. Like, prison "A" might have an HVAC vocational training course that they are interested in taking to get certified in the field. Others, and this is the majority, ask to go to certain prisons because it gets them closer to their homes and families.

When I went to sentencing, I asked the judge if he would recommend that 1 serve my time at either Bennettsville, SC or Butner, NC. He made the recommendation, but as happens so often in the federal system, that is not where I got designated. When I asked, I was told that I would be going to Beckley, W. Virginia instead.

I knew where Beckley was, since I had been through there numerous times, traveling up and down 1-77 as a truck driver. The only problem I had with going to Beckley, really, was that it was so far away from my family. Bennettsville would have put me only thirty minutes from home. Butner would have put me two and a half hours away. Unfortunately, I would not be going to either of these places so I just trusted in God that He was sending me where He needed me.

Leaving the transfer center was pretty much the same procedure as arriving, only in reverse. After being re-cuffed, re-shackled, and rechained, we were all loaded back onto the plane and told to strap in.

I could see that it was raining out that morning so I knew the flight was going to most likely be a little rougher than the flight in.

I was right about the flight. It was rough, and there was a lot of rain and lightening. We never flew above the clouds this time so my only view out the window was that of the middle of the storm. Just like my life had been for so long.

As I stared at the rain running down my window, I thought of what the sunlit cloud tops had looked like when I first flew on Con-Air.

It was so amazingly beautiful. When thinking of what Heaven must look like, I always to this day recall that scene; being totally illuminated, no shadows or darkness anywhere in sight.

We finally broke out of the clouds and began to descend. The browns and greens of the mountainous landscape below began to take shape and come into focus as we made a banking turn. Our smooth turn was interrupted quite rudely, however, by a sudden cross-wind gust that caused us to drop and shake enough to make everyone a little nervous. Since most of us on that plane had not accumulated very many air miles up to that point, there were many gasps and exclamations of surprise by the sudden and unexpected movements of the plane.

As we straightened out and began our drop to the runway, it seemed to me that we were going a little too fast, and that there was no way the pilot was going to be able to stop such a huge aircraft on such a short runway. Not at the speed we anyway. I must not have been the only one thinking this because I heard a high-pitched squeal coming from someone. In truth, I could have been that "someone" but I think it was the guy in front of me.

The wheels touched down, and when they did, everyone was thrown forward in their seats, and the plane abruptly came to a halt. One of the guards, a younger female who was always saying and doing things in front of the older, male guards to try to appear "cute" was tossed onto the floor because, instead of being buckled in, she was sitting sideways in her seat with her feet across the lap of the guard beside her, who DID have his seat belt on.

The plane pulled off the runway at the end of the strip, and then we were almost instantly swarmed by buses, vans, and cars that were there to pickup and drop off prisoners. We were called off the plane by name, then once off, we were separated into groups and load into vehicles. Which vehicle you were told to get into depended on where you were going.

I was told to board a bus with about twenty-five other men, one of which I was not entirely sure WAS a man, if you know what I mean.

We rode for about an hour and a half before finally reaching the prison called FCI-Beckley. We pulled up in front of the place and I looked out and saw that the place was surrounded by, not one, but two high fences with rows upon rows of stranded coils of razor wire. I swallowed the lump in my throat and thought, "Oh Lord, where have these people brought me?"

Under extremely heavy guard, we were escorted into the front of the building and taken to a large holding area. This is where we were once again un-cuffed and whatnot. Through the booking-in process, again, made me wonder why the jails, detention centers, transfer centers, and places like that did not just share all of this info with one another so that we could all save time and energy. This is the age of computers, after all.

The officers were calling everyone up, one at a time, to get their pictures taken for their ID cards. As I was stepping away, the officer stopped me and pointed me towards another cell. I went where he instructed and found myself locked in a smaller holding cell than the last one I was in. This one, however, only had myself and three other guys in it so we actually had more room to move around while we waited.

Eventually, a female guard came by and gave each of us a pair of new boxers (every other place we had been to only gave you used clothing. Socks and boxers included), a t-shirt, pair of green pants, a pair of socks, and a pair of slip-on shoes. We were then told, unnecessarily I might add, to get dressed and standby. We did as instructed.

Within a few minutes, another guard came and unlocked the cell door. We were lead through several more locked doors, back the way we had come earlier, after getting off of the bus. As we reached the end of that hallway, we were each handed our ID cards and mesh bags which contained two blankets, two sheets, one pillow, one pillow case, and six rolls of toilet paper along with a hygiene kit of toothpaste, toothbrush, soap, towels and wash cloths.

Mesh bags in hand, and ID cards clipped to our t-shirts, the four of us were instructed to go out front and wait. Emerging from the front door of the building, the first things we noticed was that the bus was gone and there were no heavily armed guards anywhere to be seen. We all looked at each other and asked, "You think we were supposed to come out this door?"

While we were trying to figure out how we had just gotten outside of a prison without any supervision at all, a white pickup truck pulled to the curb in front of us. An inmate, dressed all in green, got out and called for us to come over to where he was. I was reluctant, feeling like this was some kind of setup or something, but the inmate with the truck assured us that he was sent to pick us up and take us over to the camp. Not knowing what else to do, we decided to go against our better judgment and trust an inmate. Two at a time, he drove us over to the front office of the camp.

Upon arriving at the camp, the driver told us to go in the office building he had stopped in front of. In there, we were given our housing and bed assignments. After being pointed in the general direction of the unit I was being assigned to, I was sent on my way.

As I walked to the unit, I took a minute to look around. There was no fence around the place, and inmates were walking around everywhere.

I saw no guards anywhere, other than the office building I had first entered. There were a lot of trees around also, giving the place more of a college feel than a prison feel. I thought to myself, "This ain't so bad after all." And it wasn't.

I went into the building and someone helped me find my room. These rooms are not actually "rooms," and they are not cells either. They are called "cubes" because that is basically what they are; cubicles. I put my stuff on my bed and decided to go explore my surroundings. It had been a long time since I was able to move around freely so I could not wait to get outside and breathe "free" air.

One of the first things I checked out was the recreation yard. There were people walking and running on the gravel track that, surrounded the yard. There was a flag-football game in progress, as well as a basketball game that was being played on one of the two asphalt basketball courts. There were people pitching horse shoes, and a few playing bocce ball. Several people were working out, doing pushups, sit ups, and lifting bags with rocks in them. There were no weights so people were using what they had available.

I found the library in a long building that takes up one whole end of the camp area. Other things in this building included the barbershop, commissary, chow hall, medical, education, and the chapel, as well as an indoor recreation area that had pool tables and cardio exercise equipment in it. There was even a music room with drums and guitars in it for inmate use. I was feeling a little better about where I was, even if it was not where I wanted to be.

T. M. Rain and Michael Hall

CHAPTER SIXTEEN

I eventually started making my way out to the recreation yard so that I could walk the track for exercise. I had spent way too long being locked up in places where I could not go out and just walk. Losing myself in the sights, smells, and sounds of nature.

One day, while out walking, I was approached by two other inmates. One fellow was very large and dark headed while the other was of average build, and had white hair. They spoke first, introducing themselves as Steve and Mack, respectively. We exchanged a few pleasantries, laying the groundwork for what would develop into a long friendship between the three of us.

The most important thing that we all had in common, and it became apparent quickly, was that we all had a great amount of faith in Jesus Christ. Steve and Mack told me they were

Christians upon introducing themselves, and that was welcome news since I was new and did not know what kinds of people I would be meeting here. I guess I had watched too many prison movies in the past and thought everyone would be like the prisoners the actor portrayed.

The guys told me that they, along with a lot of the other Christian brothers, got together every Thursday evening for what they termed "Praise and Worship." I was invited to attend, and I promised that I would and thanked them for inviting me.

That day, as we talked, we began walking around the track. I shared with them how God had been using me along my journey through the seemingly endless string of jails and holding centers- Steve asked me if I would mind sharing my story with the rest of the guys at the next evening meeting. I said that I would be more than happy to do just that.

From Prison to Praise

The night of the Praise and Worship meeting, I walked in a little nervous since I was about to meet a bunch of people for the first time. Also, I knew that Steve wanted me to share my story of how God has been doing work through me. Now, I love to talk about God, and the power He has over my life, I just get a little nervous standing up in front of new people to speak. I never know if the meaning of what I want to say is going to come through the way I want it to or not. So, walking into that room that evening, I just took a deep breath and trusted in God to give me the words I needed to let these guys know I was for real, and not a jailhouse religion fake.

Steve was with me that night when I walked to the chapel- Mack was not. We walked in and there was about fifteen people sitting around in these blue plastic chairs. One old guy was holding a guitar, and another skinny fellow was holding a banjo. A third guy with long dark hair held a mandolin. Mack eventually came in carrying yet another guitar.

Over the next several minutes, a few others came in and finally Steve got up and started the evening's service. He began with a prayer then he handed it over to the older guy with the guitar. His name was John.

John told us what song he had chosen, and as we opened our books to the correct page the music began. I was really amazed at how good the music and the voices blended and sounded in that small area. My spirit leapt within me as we praised God together in song.

After singing a couple more songs, there was a lull in the events. Everyone was quietly sitting in their chairs, as if lost in their own thoughts for the moment. I sat there, feeling the love and energy that seemed to fill the room. Suddenly, the silence was broken by a strong baritone voice singing "Beulah Land," without any musical accompaniment at all. We all sat and listened, then joined in on the chorus.

The voice behind the song was Mack. This was his "signature song," although he knew and sang many more just as well.

Following this song, Steve stood up and introduced me to the group, and asked me to step to the front of the room and share something with them. By this point in the evening, r had lost my nervousness completely, or, most likely/ it had been removed by God as I had ask Him to help me this evening.

That night I expressed to everyone how Christ was the center of my life. I said that, in the past, I had been like Jonah. I had tried going in directions contrary to His leading. I said that I felt like this time of incarceration was like me being in the belly of the whale. I had been surrounded by things that were rotten and sickening because I. had been obstinate, wanting to do things MY way.

I let them know that, like He had with them, God had finally gotten my full attention- He has shown me a better Way, and although some people will probably never understand how me being in prison can be considered a blessing from God, I did, and I still do to this day.

After sharing a few more words of encouragement with my new friends, I thanked them then returned to my seat. We sang again to close out the service, then dismissed with a prayer. Afterward, Steve and Mack walked me back to my building. Along the way, I told Mack how much I had enjoyed the evening's events, and especially his song. Steve told me that he was impressed by what I had shared with them, and how open I had been. I told him that I had just said what God had put in my heart to share.

From the first moment I met my first roommate, I knew that things were not going to work out, but I hoped we would grow on one another over time. When I got back from the Praise and Worship service, he was waiting for me in our cube. It was very apparent from the look he gave me when I walked in that I was not what he considered to be an acceptable roommate.

My roommate and I were complete opposites, in every way. He was a young black man, standing close to 6'4", or more. I am a short, older, white dude. One of the first things he told me was that he did not like old guys, especially white ones. He further informed me that night that he was a Muslim, and he did not want to share his space with an "infidel."

No, this was not going to work out; for either of us.

The older guy who had been playing the guitar at the meeting lived just a couple of cubes down from me. He heard the comments that were made. He called me down to his cube and told me not to pay any attention to that guy. He told me that I should ask to be moved into his cube, since he did not have a roommate at the time.

The next morning, I went to my counselor's office to get my

necessary numbers that I would need for using the phones, and for various other reasons. I learned quickly that, in federal prison, I was nothing but a number in the crowd. To staff, I was "Inmate Hall," followed by my federal register number. While I was there, I asked the counselor to be moved into a different cube. He told me it was no problem, and asked which cube I wanted to move to. I told him. After a few pecks on the keyboard, he told me to go ahead and move. Simple as that, and with no questions asked.

My new roommate was very helpful in helping me settle in, and making sure I had all of the necessities for survival, you could say. I was given a pair of Reeboks with a little life left in them, and a sweat suit. Well, a pair of sweat pants actually, not the whole sweat suit, but it was great to have them to wear around the recreation yard. I was also given a bowl, cup, and fork and spoon for using in the unit. Probably the best thing I was given that day was a bar of "real" soap and shampoo. After using jail issued stuff for so long, this felt more like being at home. Hey, maybe you don't understand it but this is something big to people like me so try not to think I am too crazy for getting excited over some soap

One thing that I had learned during my incarceration up until this point is that, no matter where you are at, things get a whole lot easier once you have a normal routine established. It was going to be no different here at Beckley. The first thing you have to figure out when trying to get your daily routine started is, what is the prison's daily routine?

In the federal prison system, just like in any prison system, they count several times per day. We are counted on weekdays at 12:00am, 3:00am, 5:00am, 4:00pm, and then at 10:00pm. On the weekends, they throw in another count at 10:00am. Of course there are also counts thrown in from time to time to see if everyone is where they are supposed to be. If you have a job, and are supposed to be there, that is where you had better be if they pop up with one of these counts.

Our meals are served on a schedule as well. Breakfast starts at 6:00am, and this is when you also go to drop off you dirty laundry. Lunch is served at 10:30am, and supper is served sometime between 4:30pm and 5:00pm or whenever count is cleared.

Another rule is that, unless we are on the recreation yard, we are required to wear our "greens," as our green uniforms are called. We are not required to wear them on weekends or holidays, unless we are working on one of those days, which some people, like the kitchen workers do.

I was happy to learn from my new friends, Steve and Mack, that Beckley had a very well established religious program in place. And, they informed me, there were several volunteers who came in one their own time, all during the week, to help people study and learn, and to preach God's good word.

Saturday mornings had some really great Bible teaching, which was lead by a local pastor. This pastor was usually accompanied by his neighbor who also worked at the church taking care of the office affairs. This was Dave.

On Saturday afternoons, three ladies came in with music and a message. They were from a local Pentecostal-type church where they wore long dresses, no makeup, and no jewelry. The oldest of the ladies (she must have been pushing 80 years old, if not older) would often break loose, and start dancing. She would hold her hands up high, and she would start singing and praying in tongues.

On Sundays, after lunch, a couple of guys would come in and teach on the Old Testament. Their focus was usually on the tabernacle, and what all the different things meant. After supper on Sunday evenings, we would have our weekly chapel service. This service was lead by the chaplain who actually worked for the Bureau of Prisons (BOP).

The BOP chaplain has a lot of duties. He is not only responsible for all of the religious activities at the camp, where I am, but he is also responsible for all of the religious activities at the medium security facility next door, or "behind the fence" as we call it- I will also note that he is responsible for overseeing ALL of the various religions, but more on that in a minute.

On two Mondays each month, a pastor from a local church would come in and teach a very energetic Bible study. On another Monday during the month, another guy came in to teach lessons on varying topics from the Bible. The other Monday, three or four guys came with a mostly musical service. They would play and sing, then they would teach a short, 5-10 minutes, message of encouragement. On Thursday nights, two times each month, a fellow from an independent Baptist church would drive about an hour and a half to bring us a message that was usually closed with an alter call.

As I said earlier, the BOP chaplain is responsible for overseeing all religious activities, for all religions. This means he is the one who has to arrange for the volunteers to come in, arrange the schedules, and the meeting places. And, he has to make sure that all religions are taken care of, no matter what his feelings on their personal beliefs might be.

There were Catholic services held on Sunday also. There are provisions made for the Native Americans so that they had their own area where they have a "sweat lodge," as most people call it. The Muslim group has Friday afternoon prayers, and the Jewish community has accommodations for their various observances throughout the year. At the time of this writing, Beckley camp has had a few Pagans arrive and they have had a worship area set up for their rituals and worship. There are Wiccans as well as Asatru, and they share, by mutual agreement, the same area, just their worship days are separate.

Steve told me about all of the different groups when I first got here, but it was pretty apparent to me from the beginning that the Christian group was the most dominate one on the compound. Therefore, we had the most volunteers coming in, and we were allotted a majority of the chapel time.

My roommate, John, spent a lot of his time in the music room, where he would join others to play and sing together. One day I was sitting there listening to them when suddenly John asked me if I had been looking for a job. I told him that, in all honesty, I had not. He told me that it would probably be in my best interest if I found one pretty quick, before "they" gave me one I would not like. "They" being my counselor or case manager.

John introduced me to one of his friends, Greg, who was also sitting there that day. Greg was a chapel orderly and he would be going home soon, John said. I talked to Greg about what all his job consisted of and then told him that it sounded like something I would be interested in. Greg agreed to teach me the details of his job, then when he was about to leave, he would recommend me to the chaplain. Since I would already know the job, he did not see any reason why I would not be hired.

I was very happy with what I considered, at the time, to be the perfect job for me. All I had to do as chapel orderly really was set everything up for the various chapel services, and keep the chapel clean and in good order. These duties included sweeping, mopping, dusting, and keeping all of the books, DVDs, and VHS tapes in their correct places. If any of the books were damaged, it was also part of my job to repair them, if it was possible. If not, I was to give the damaged book to the chaplain so that it could be replaced.

Once Greg felt like I was capable of handling the job on my own, we went to speak to the chaplain about the job. I was told by the chaplain that I could in fact have the job, and that I could start immediately.

The only problem, he explained, was that I could not officially go on the payroll until after Greg left. That was more than fine with me, and I thanked the chaplain for the job. Needless to say, I was delighted!

Praise God! I could not help but think. Things were falling into place for me. I was getting a daily routine down, and time would soon start to fly by for me. That is all any of us here in prison can really ask for.

I loved my job so much that, at the end of the day, I could not wait until the next morning when I could go back to work. Working as the chapel orderly was my "job," but it was not work. I wanted to be there, in a place where people who loved God came to worship, or sometimes just to ask questions.

The only time I ever had trouble at work was when I had to set up for the catholic services. Let me re-phrase that; the only time I did not really know what I needed to do on a regular basis was when I had to set up for the Catholic services. There were so many books, candles, tables, and chairs, and they all had to be arranged in a certain way.

Which way always depended on which priest was going to be there on any particular night. Usually, I just waited for the priest to show up so I could just ask him what he needed me to do.

When the Sister came, she always wanted the chairs arranged in a circle with hers facing the door. No tables or candles.

I got my first look into a lot of these different religions by coming to work in the chapel. I was learning that, along with a lot of the differences, there were also a lot of similarities between most religions. Including Christianity.

CHAPTER SEVENTEEN

After I had been at Beckley for a couple of months, I was happily surprised when my family informed me that they were going to be able to make the trip up to see me. This was wonderful news. No longer would our visits include trying to speak to one another through a thick pane of glass, and only for a few minutes at a time for that matter. This time we would get to spend the whole day together.

The day of the visit came. I was up and ready when my name was called over the intercom system at about 8:00am. When I walked into the visiting room, I greeted each of my family members with a quick hug and kiss, as was allowed by BOP policy. We sat and visited for hours, although it seemed like only minutes. At 3:00pm, they had to leave. Since the trip was so long, they decided to stay the night in a motel then come back the next day. That visit went by just as fast as the day before.

I called my wife's cell phone at around 9:00pm to make sure they were making it home safely. She said they were almost home, and had had no problems. I was thankful to the Lord for that.

The next day, I was still flying high from my visits, and of course I was praising God for letting it happen. That visit was something I had been praying for.

It is really easy to praise God when things are all working out favorably for you. The challenge comes when things start going wrong, or at least when they appear to be going wrong. As good as my visit was, it also set off a chain of events that I did not see coming until it was too late.

During my visit with my family, my wife was telling me about someone from back home who had moved to West Virginia recently to be the pastor of a church that was located somewhere in or around Beckley. Neither she nor I knew him personally, but I told her that I would ask one of the local volunteers if perhaps one of them knew or knew of this person.

Being very "green" when it came to the policies here, I wrote the pastors name on a piece of paper and gave it to one of the volunteers when he came in one night. I asked if he knew the guy, but he did not.

Then I asked if he would mind checking the local directory to see if the guy was listed. The volunteer asked me why I was so curious about this person and I explained to him how my wife had been told about him moving from where we are from to this area. I also told him that since we had an opening for a new volunteer, this guy, or someone he knew, might be interested in filling the gap. He just nodded then pocketed the piece of paper.

About a week passed and I had not heard anything back from

the volunteer. Then one day I got called to come to the chaplain's office.

I walked over to the office, and as soon as I had walked in and sat down, the chaplain asked me what I thought I was doing? I had no idea what he was talking about, but I could tell that he was very angry over something, and it was pretty obvious that "something" was something I had done wrong.

I told the chaplain that I was not sure what he meant, and ask if he would be a little more specific. He started explaining to me that, by passing the volunteer a note, I had completely jeopardized the privileges of that volunteer, and the whole volunteer program. I told him that I had not actually passed the volunteer a note. I had simply given him a name that I had written down on a piece of paper. He said that it did not matter, inmates are not allowed to pass anything to volunteers, and they are not allowed to accept anything that someone tries to pass them.

If an inmate tries to pass something to a volunteer, that person is to report the incident immediately, which, I supposed, is what had happened here in my case.

I spent quite a long while in that office apologizing to the chaplain.

I explained to him that I had not been made aware of this policy, and I certainly meant no harm by making my request the way I did. I also assured him that it would never happen again. The next time I saw the volunteer I apologized to him as well, telling him also that I had not known of the policy, or otherwise I would have never handed him anything.

A couple of weeks passed, and I started thinking it was all water under the bridge. Then, one afternoon, I was called into an office to be interviewed by SIS, which is the investigative department within the prison. They served me with an incident report, or a write-up, which is the beginning of the disciplinary process. After I was handed the incident report, I was taken away to the SHU, which stands for; special housing unit. You might have heard it referred to as "The Hole." I would be staying here until the disciplinary process was over.

I knew the other guy in my cell. He was in there because he had been involved in a fight over the television; a common occurrence in prison, unfortunately.

After a while, I asked my roommate, "Bo," about his personal religious beliefs. He told me that he had trouble believing in a god who would allow such terrible things to happen in a world He supposedly loved so much. Bo told me that he had asked several "Jesus freaks" why He would do such a thing, and he had never been given an acceptable answer. That, he said, was the only thing that really stood in the way of him believing.

Silently calling upon the Lord to give me the right words to reach this man, I found myself asking him if he had any children at home. He said that he had a son, and he said that he planned on living with him when he got out in a couple of months. As he talked, I could tell that his son was everything to him. When he stopped talking, I asked Bo if he would be willing to give his son's life to save the life of a stranger.

"No way," he quickly responded.

When I asked why not, he said, "Someone still has to die. If it comes down to my son, or someone else's, well it's not going to be mine. Not if I can help it."

I began to explain to him about how God had given each and every one of us free will. What we choose to do with it is entirely up to us. Unfortunately, I said, some people would rather chose to do evil than to do good. Sure, I explained further, God could take our free will away from us, if he really wanted to. Then no one would ever do anything terrible to anyone else. The down side to that however is, taking away our freedom to choose right or wrong, good or evil, would basically reduce us to nothing more than robots or puppets.

I asked Bo if he knew what the John 3:16, that God so loved the world that He gave His ONLY begotten son... His ONLY son, I asked. Bo said that he knew the verse. Then I asked him if he realized that God loved HIM so much, even thousands of years before he was even born, that He sent His son to this world so that he could one day have everlasting life. All he had to do was believe in the sacrifice made by Jesus, and accent Him as his Lord and Savior. That ended our little conversation right then and there. Bo said he was tired, and he was going to bed.

That night, before I went to sleep, I prayed and thanked God for the words He had given me. I also asked Him to work on Bo, to try to change his heart and the way he looks at what goes on in the world. I asked that Bo be given understanding. Then I went to sleep.

The next morning, Bo woke me up for breakfast. Breakfast comes early in the SHU and I was only about half awake as I ate. When Bo looked at me and said, "You can go back to the camp now, you have accomplished what you came over here to do," I was not sure I had heard him correctly. I asked him for clarification. Bo said that he had not been able to sleep all night because he kept thinking about everything I had told him. What he had heard kept replaying over and over in his mind, and just before they brought the breakfast trays, he had called upon Jesus to come into his heart and be his Lord and Savior.

I was stunned and happy, all at the same time. Tears rolled down his cheeks as he told me about what had transpired inside him during the night. He asked me if I thought God would hold it against him that he had doubted Him the way he had for so long. I told him that, once he accepted Jesus into his life, all had been forgiven.

A couple of days later, they moved Bo out and moved a young African American fellow named Brown in with me. Brown, it turned out, was related to one of the officers working at the institution, and policy stated that they could not be on the same compound. Brown was being locked up in the SHU to await transfer to another facility.

I spend most of my waking hours reading a Bible the chaplain had dropped off for me during one of his regular visits to see the guys who are "locked up," as we say. The SHU is considered jail for those in jail. It is a running joke in about every jail or prison that, when someone is doing something that is against the rules, or might just get on the officers nerves, and someone points it out, the person might say, "What are they going to do, put me in jail?"

Anyway, when I asked about what Browns religion was, he told me that he had never really been around ANY religion before, and he just figured that you had to make the most out of what you had, while you had it.

He was not against religion, he explained. He had just never been involved in one enough to really have any kind of belief system or ©pinions in the matter.

I tried to give him a quick summary of my faith. First, I told him that I believed the Bible to be the true Word of God. It was written, I explained, over a fifteen-hundred year period, by forty different authors who were scattered across three continents, yet it still had a common theme without any contradictions.

Secondly, I told him that since the first five words in the Bible were, "In the beginning God created," that told me that everything that exists today is a result, in one way or another, of the original creation. If God created something, including me, all of creation belongs to Him. With that being said, I told him, I believed it to be in my best interest to read His book, and do what He says.

I spent much time talking to Brown, explaining how God had made a way to redeem us since we were all sinners, yet He loved us still. Brown listened closely, stopping me from time to time to ask a question so that he had a better understanding of what I was telling him. The last question Brown asked me was the most important one; he wanted to know how he could get in' on the action of everlasting life? I shared with him the simple, yet profound, plan of salvation that God had made readily available to all of us through the sacrifice of His son, Jesus Christ.

Brown said that he wanted to do exactly what I had told him about. He wanted a new life, and he was more than willing to repent. Turning away from the old, and embracing the new by placing his faith and trust in the one who had died for him.

As we prayed together, he accepted Christ as his own. Inside, I was praising God once again for the opportunity to lead yet another lost soul to Him.

About a week later, I was sent back to the camp. Unfortunately, I had been gone for so long that I had to start over again with a new cellie in a new cube. My old cellie, or roommate, and I were only separated by one cube. He and I got to talking about what had happened and he asked again Why I was here? He meant at Beckley, but that was not how I answered him. I told John that I believed I was brought here by divine appointment. He thought this was humorous, and he chuckled a little and said, "Right."

I guess that since John played and sang in the chapel, I just assumed his faith was ad strong as the rest of the men's in the group. This, as it turned out, was not exactly the case. Maybe I should have known better, after having lived with him for a while.

I started talking to John about his faith, and sharing with him how God had used me during my time in the "bucket," another pet-name for the SHU. I told him how I had the opportunity to help two men find their way to salvation while I was there. I also told John that I loved him like a brother, and I would like to know for sure of his relationship with the Lord. He started telling me that he felt like he would be alright because he had asked God to forgive him for the drugs and women and such, as he put it.

I asked John if he realized that he was a sinner, and that ONLY Jesus' finished work on the cross could pay his debt. I explained to him that he had to repent and ask Jesus into his life, and live by the faith in the finished work on the cross.

John thought about what I had said, and a few days later, as we were talking again, he shared with me that he had had a long talk with "the man upstairs," and gotten everything taken care of with him.

John began attending the teaching and worship services, as well as the singing parts of our fellowships. When his day finally came to leave here and go to the halfway-house in Kentucky, I walked him down to the discharge area. We have remained in contact ever since then, and I have seen God's blessing in his life as he met and then married a Christian widow. They moved to Florida and have prospered in so many ways. At 74 years of age, he is doing what he enjoys most; playing guitar and singing.

From time to time, John gets together with others to play music. He often gets to play for people in a retirement home. He also no longer thinks my statement about being sent here by divine appointment is funny, in fact, he has confirmed and agreed with me that God hap sent me here for a reason.

One of the greatest blessings for me while I have been here has been through the great Bible teaching from Pastor Don. He has taught us the "greatness of the Kingdom" (Book from seminary by: Alva McLean) over a period of many months. He inspired me to seek out the scriptures to see what God is saying to me in them.

Pastor Don taught with such a style as to lead you to the truth through a series of questions and answers. He brought you to the truth by progression that way. Not only would you get the answers to the questions you might have, or the ones he might have asked you, but he taught you a path for finding the answers yourself. This was a path you could use for the rest of your life.

We often looked at controversial issues of faith where he

would present the various opposing views, listing the strong points, as well as the weaknesses, of the arguments. The group would be able to interact, asking questions and making comments of our own. He was very good at being able to take us directly to the Bible to support whatever he was asked to address at any given moment. On the rare occasions when he did not feel as if he were fully prepared to respond correctly, he would simply say, "Let me get back to you on that later." He was just being honest that he wanted time to be better prepared to address what was asked of him.

I was able to learn by example from him how to pass the torch of ministry as well. After pastoring for around forty years at the same church, he transitioned his replacement into place over a two year period so the "flock" would be comfortable with, and confident in, the new man of God at the helm of their church.

Twice each month, another local pastor came and led a very

strong Bible study. Brother Butch encouraged each of us that attended the study to always have our Bibles, and to take notes, which I did, and continue to do today. Brother Butch taught with a very charismatic style that would really get your attention. He used many object lessons so that we could better understand and visualize some of the principles he taught. His hope and prayer, he said, was that he might be able to say something to strengthen our faith, and encourage our relationship with the Lord.

Brother Randal also came twice each month. He had an executive-type position with a large mining company and had traveled to Germany several times. He made it clear that serving God was his first priority, family second, and the job came third. I learned a lot from that because it had not always been that way for me. I often had my priorities messed up, putting work ahead of not only God and family, but absolutely everything else in my life. Many times, there was no room at all for God.

Brother Randal usually brought a message of repentance, and he was constantly encouraging and Inviting men to become active members of the family of God. At the close of each of his messages, an alter call was always given. It was not unusual for one or two guys to come forward to make a profession of faith.

I have always considered it a privilege to be able to take a new convert and feed him on the sincere Word of God to help him grow in his new faith. Not only is it a privilege, it is a responsibility.

Something interesting here at Beckley is that we also have a good amount of video teaching in the chapel. We have studied through a presentation of Creation Science Evangelism, consisting of seven DVDs that presented evidence of a global flood, and a relatively young Earth; less than 10,000 years as opposed to the belief in the theory of evolution which puts it at billions of years old.

We have studied a 12 session series called "The Truth Project" in which Dr. Del Tackett presents many fundamental truths of scripture for us to build upon.

There are many more of these types of teachings we are blessed to have to learn from. Most are from very well known men such as John Piper, R.C. Sproul, Dan Hayden, John McAuthor, and Ken Hamm, just to name a few.

During my time here, it has been my great privilege to teach weekly Bible study groups. When teaching, it is very important to me that I am able to show that, in any of my opinions, I am always standing on the side of truth. Rightly dividing the scriptures as a whole, and not simply finding an isolated verse or phrase, to support my thoughts and beliefs.

As I look back over the last five years that I have been here, I praise God for the good that has come of it. There have been personal struggles that I have had to deal with along the way. The enemy of my soul, Satan, attacks me in my most vulnerable areas. I have dealt with attacks from the assurance of my salvation to my family suffering due to my absence. During the last three years I have been trying to have my case revisited by the courts. At every turn, I have been blocked from having the issues in my case addressed. The prosecutor's office has used every roadblock they can throw up to keep the core issue from being heard.

I continue to file with the courts to get my "day in Court," but it does get frustrating sometimes because, if I were to be successful with my appeal, I would receive immediate release from custody. This is where faith comes in. I have a promise from God in Romans 8:28 that *"all things work together for good for them that are the called according to His purpose."*

Maybe God is not finished with me here. Maybe there is more meant for me to do in order to serve Him. I do not know, but I will not lose sight of the fact that I made a promise to do God's work, and I will do it; no matter where that work needs to be done. I do take encouragement from Proverbs 3:5-6 where I am told,

> *"Trust in the Lord with all your heart and lean not to your own understanding, but in all ways acknowledge Him and He will direct your paths."*

No, I do not know what tomorrow holds, but I have full confidence that God is able to keep me, and has the power to remove me from this place whenever, and however, He chooses. He has already released me from the bondage of sin and put a song in my heart. There is nothing more powerful than Him and His love.

My hope and prayer for the future is to go back home, and to tell others of the great things God has done for me. I want to be a living testament to His compassion, and to present His invitation of deliverance and salvation to others. That is my greatest desire in life. I pray for an opportunity to serve in a full time ministry one day, also.

I have a growing family I want to be once again united with, and to become re-acquainted with as well. Being apart from them for very long, and only getting to see some of them once a year, has really put a strain on all of us.

My youngest son, Dylan, once told me by phone, "Dad, being grown up ain't what it's talked up to be. Sometimes I wish I was a little boy again, and could just climb up in your lap, and you could hold me and assure me everything is going to be alright."

I hope to be able to impart, not only to my son, but to everyone

I can, that we all have a Father in Heaven that awaits with open arms for us to come running to Him. This is the victory that I have in Him as my Lord and Savior because He has brought me out of the bondage of sin, and into His daily presence, with thanks giving on this journey from prison to praise.

ABOUT THE AUTHORS

T.M. Rain and Michael Hall are both currently incarcerated for drug conspiracy charges. Although some might think of this time in their lives as dark or depressing, the authors want to use the time to spread the word of God's love, and of His work that is being done inside prison walls.

This is their first book, and they hope you enjoy it and are able to take something positive away from reading it.

T. M. Rain and Michael Hall

Manufactured by Amazon.ca
Acheson, AB

32594764R00149